WHY I THINK EVERYONE SHOULD SMOKE CIGARETTES: THE CURE TO POSTMODERNISM

Volume III: War

Ernesto Castelli

Born to Feel

CONTENTS

AMERICAN PSYCHO AND WHY NOTHING EVER HAPPENS

Leafing through old comic books my Italian uncle left me when I was younger, I came across, in the white cardboard box with push in handles I bought at the comic book store in Brookline, MA that was recently replaced by a newer, upscale one, a series of Batman comics. I flipped through the orange newspaper inked pages of issues 445-447 where graphic design principles created for such proportioned pages still gave meaning, structure, and style to an American life and the design aesthetic requiring it. American soldiers and athletes sold as trading cards, video games, and action figures reflected American values across the page from communist KGB conservationists in orange masks ready to be defeated by Batman and his American values. Soldiers can be bought and sold as video games and action figures, but seldom trading cards, athletes rarely action figures, and superheroes all three. TikTok ads and art school have yet to catch up to the graphic design principles of this era of American marketing, a platform and advertising style desperately necessary for the digital age simply ignored by the private corporations wishing to use bland AI instead of young internet based artists for advertising. Written in 1990 during a time when Italian Americans still held prominent roles in American artistry, Batman is enlisted by Commissioner Gordon to take out an ex-KGB soldier seeking to take revenge on the newly minted, free trade friendly Russian regime. Ushered in by the woman Bruce Wayne dates while in

Russia, her conversation with Wayne breaks the seal between Russian and American relations. Mary Wolfman has Anna say, when speaking of Russia:

"Beautiful *country filled with beautiful people. And they're* nothing *like what I expected. [...] Different value system.* [Americans] *assume everyone is* motivated *by personal achievement, but here there really* is *a sense of* group effort. *No classes. No distinctions. They'd be* uncomfortable *with someone like [Bruce Wayne] -- an* ordinary *citizen with incredible* wealth."[1]

As Svetlana Boym argued, Russian culture, unlike Western and particularly American culture, was never about the private vs. public life - it was about the material vs. immaterial, the spiritual creation of what it means to be Russian, not the consumption patterns that create Americans.[2] It is inside this conflict that we see Batman duke it out with the *KGB*east. The communist's lifestyle has no public or private distinction - much like the heart of the Russian motherland, the spiritual transformation communism gave its people, that of taking peasantry and turning them into noblemen through the slaughter of the innocent or the bourgeois, is the *KGB*east's own personal mission, for himself and his people, against Batman and the American lifestyle ushered in by global trade. In private, the beast worships Lenin as he does in public - his tension lies not between these realities, as it does for Bruce Wayne and his public persona, Batman, but in the spiritual transformation being the Beast represents for him and his people.[3] Bruce, of course, has nothing of this to deal with - he keeps his identity as Batman hidden from his lover, as all Western gentlemen must do, as his private and public life are kept comfortably separate, the resoundingly British worldbuilding of Batman's gothic exterior and lifestyle never interfering with his American business relations. Batman, and Wayne of course, prevail against the *KGB*east in the final issue, the word "prevail" in this sentence highlighting how despite speaking of the same man, we treat Bruce Wayne and Batman as equals. Unable to kill his communist opponent, a Russian armed forces operative kills the beast in Batman's place. The question that Batman, and his world, poses for his readers, is not that of Bruce Wayne's, or of Batman's morality, but of the actions our private selves have on our public ones. Batman would not be Batman if it were not for Bruce Wayne, nor would the Scarecrow be the Scarecrow were it not for his private persona - the beauty of Alan Moore's <u>Watchmen</u> is in its ability to blur this line between the private and public selves, so that, unlike in Bruce Wayne's world, the truth of our lives, that we are more informed by our public selves in our private lives than the other way around, may arise. Perhaps this is why Kanye West and Donald Trump have so often been reduced to lunatics, and why the only true villain in Batman's world is the Joker - for to take joy in the lunacy of it all, as the Joker does, is to have no distinction between your public and private self in the first place. The question, after all, of, *"but what are they like in private?"* is at the heart of all cancel culture missions, each one seeking to create a spiritual conquest, and revival, of our own collective failed consciousness as, in our own private places, we seek to, in denying others of their own, gain a sense of self, and morality, over those who chose to make themselves public in the first place - as if we could ourselves handle that scrutiny. It is not that the personal is political, as Western thinkers may have you believe, but that the outstanding morality of the few and the brave we can venerate is so monstrous we forget that we were not supposed to have a public, or personal life, to begin with.

It is within this tension, amongst others, that the film *American Psycho* takes place. Now adopted by men, who much like the Joker, are labeled insane for keeping what most men consider their private views on women public on sites like 4chan or X, formerly known as Twitter, incels have

"Memed [Patrick Bateman] to the point of being recognized by zoomers who have never seen the movie as a sigma male grindset rich guy instead of a serial killer".

-Anon

Utterly poetic in tone, *American Psycho*'s re-appropriation in American life as someone stickin' it to the man through desperate cries for help through his own self-conscious postmodern irony is about as Gen Z as you can get. *American Psycho* begins, following the practice Cormac McCarthy lays out in his novel <u>Blood Meridian</u>: by letting blood in a swank Manhattan restaurant with saturated pink and green hues as food comes to represent phallic and vaginal psychosexual imagery exceedingly sociopathic and heterosexual in tone. The colors of the movie are always fully saturated; blues are always blue, and reds are always red. Jews are brought up alongside banks as their place in America becomes impossible to criticize; waiters, the second of whom have brown skin tone, walk gayly in the "women's restaurant" impossible to enjoy by Manhattan bankers in grey suits. A dark night club is the setting of the first killing as the film cuts away from steel credit cards on top of copper plates to a club gate kept by a black pirate with lipstick as Patrick Bateman deals with the frustration of the meaninglessness of women in his society. Bateman's apartment, the dream of all 27 year olds, is depicted violently, the furniture and structure of the living situation psychopathically depicted as Bateman's routine, despite "masculine" in products and tone, is decidedly feminine, or as others would call it, that of a gay man's. Much like the women in Lacan's philosophy, Bateman simply does not exist - he is an empty vessel filled with objects meant to represent masculinity. When he looks at the women in his life he only sees the reflection of his own revenge, disdain, and frustration as to the meaninglessness of the power he holds over women in his social and professional life - he is, in many ways, a gay man pretending to be straight. The movie begins, and its first murder, occurs when Bateman is encountered with this side of himself that he is forbidden, by society, to allow.

"*A ceremony then. One could well argue that there are not categories of no ceremony but the only ceremonies of greater or lesser degree and deferring to this argument we will say that this is a ceremony of certain magnitude perhaps more commonly called a ritual. A ritual includes a letting of blood. Rituals that fail in this requirement are false rituals.*"[4]

"Suddenly one of the gypsies, in trembling opal, seizes a cocktail out of the air, dumps it down for courage and, moving her hands like Frisco, dances out alone on the canvas platform. A momentary hush; the orchestra leader varies his rhythm obligingly for her, and there is a burst of chatter as the erroneous news goes around that she is Gilda Gray's understudy from the Follies. *The party has begun.*

I believe that on the first night I went to Gatsby's house I was one of the few guests who had actually been invited. People were not invited - they went there."[5]

Taking out his stress on his first murder victim, Bateman's self-conscious irony pervades his dialogues as his attempts and analyses of power that necessitate his domination over other men through women sit in the foreground as pornography plays in the background. He looks at his own lack of self control in life as he tries to figure out what masculinity even means while contemplating the woman on the cover of his Inside Lydia's Ass VHS tape as Donald Trump's adoration of white American women through the love he makes to pornstars becomes clear. Restaurants become means to an end to fit in as he has an affair with his friend's fiance hopped up on different drugs than him as she looks internally for solutions through medication and he does externally through workout routines, musical knowledge, and sex tapes. A woman cries out for a baby as she comes to represent the city of New York itself crying out for help while Bateman ignores her for his own reflection in the taxi cab window.

The psychosexual becomes realized as food becomes a way to give a woman subdued under opiates an orgasm in capitalist America and men display phallic symbols of violence and supremacy through suits, ties, and a taste in off-whites and European fonts that would make even a woman jealous. Bateman's next victim, a homeless man on the street, is subjected to violent character attacks by Bateman as Bateman sees his own vacuous existence reflected in the homeless man - he does not tell the homeless man to get a job, he tells himself. He kills the man not because of his hatred towards him, but because he himself cannot handle the aspects of himself he sees in the homeless man. Women in the film are portrayed as ignorant, or foolish, for being attracted to Bateman - it is this reflection, that of his private and public self only accessible by the women in his life, that drives him to madness, and necessitates his murder of them - he cannot handle the fact that the women he wishes to love are as trapped, and as empty, as him. Even when he tries to be serious, Bateman's irony is all pervasive as a cry for help while he restrains himself from killing the men around him. "Hip to be Square" plays as Bateman, finally releasing his rage, knows what it's like to be square, not because he returns to normalcy after killing a man, but because he is only human when he releases his stress by killing another. He is not the psychopath; it is those around him who cannot admit to being psychopaths that are truly sick.

As the detective walks in, Bateman knows, psychopathically, to speak of suits to assert his masculinity when meeting a man; the detective, hearing this, and still, as does Bateman's secretary, admiring Bateman, internalizes the statement. Bateman, shot closer than the detective and made to look small or childlike in close up shots, is contrasted against the detective by the windows with open shades that let in the sunlight and shadows of New York's skyscrapers into his office. The light emanating from Bateman's window upholds the lie he is trying to portray.

Violence, sex, and the food associated with it are blended together as Bateman scoops up a Russian prostitute from the seat of his limo. Each character is seen through each other's eyes as they see reflections of themselves in one another's gaze, his false intimacy with the street prostitute and the comments he makes about them cries for help. The prostitutes of that night care as much about his profession as he does, his necessary routine that begins with the chorus of his CD collection part of the ritual he becomes trapped in as he tries, even with prostitutes, to display his masculinity through the recreation of pornography. He becomes an artist through his sexual violence, finally becoming the ultimate sex symbol of a rock musician during a threeway where the street prostitute sees through his charade in disdain. When Bateman reunites with his male counterparts once more, he tries to keep his composure as his own irony is not enough to hold his sanity together while he tries to make up for natural male chauvinism. In the bathroom, Bateman tries to kill Lewis, the company's homosexual and dandy, before failing once Lewis tries to seduce him. Unable to admit to his own homosexuality, Lewis remains alive as Bateman says he has to return his pornographic VHS tapes as he tries to regain his masculinity without having to come into contact with his own homosexuality. As his murders intensify, so too do the women he murders come to care for him more, tender loving care becoming replaced with murder. Had Bateman been a hero, the movie would have been a tragedy, but because he is a villain, the movie is a comedy. Bateman meets with the detective once more in a restaurant where their roles and power as men are reversed as the stained glass behind the detective's seat matched by the wooden background invokes the idea of a Catholic confessional.

Bateman goes to see the prostitute on the street once more as his private life inches closer and closer to his public one. The prostitute on the street serves as an out to this dichotomy, for she has nothing to hide. Her class and her private life is conveyed at once through her profession as she represents New York's brutal reality. Invited one last time this time by Bateman into Paul Allen's apartment the prostitute is confronted with disgusting contempt for reality the rich of New York live in as Bateman discusses sex with his "friend" Christy. Bateman monologues about music once more as both women try to have sex with one another in front of him. The prostitute tries to run away from Bateman as he kills Christy in bed until he chases her into the apartment staircase and drops a chainsaw onto her.

"The room was full of people. One of the girls in yellow was playing the piano, and beside her stood a tall, red-haired young lady from a famous chorus, engaged in song. She had drunk a quantity of champagne, and during the course of her song she had decided,

ineptly, that everything was very, very sad - she was not only singing, she was weeping too. [...]

'She had a fight with a man who says he's her husband,' explained a girl at my elbow."[6]

Finally breaking all hopes of remaining sanity, Bateman can no longer hold back violent urges in public as, in killing the prostitute, he has killed a woman, who much like him, knows how deeply trapped he is in New York society. He wishes death to yuppies as he continues to use irony to blend in with them as his cries for help, ironic or direct, are impossible for them to validate as their private lives are as sinful and vindictive as his own. Fleeing from the police, all attempts at sincerity or sentimentality to represent a clean American life are met with death at Bateman's hands, his need for control only satisfied by his urge to destroy that which forces him into a state of ironic self preservation. Breaking down over the phone and finally displaying his humanity to his society, he confesses his murders over the phone to his lawyer as, in his need for a witness, he chose extreme violence so he could validate his own reality.

As he goes back to Paul Allen's apartment, he finds it in the process of being renewed. Its walls have been painted over to represent the purity of the America he was hoping to escape from, the bodies of the women he killed hanging in the closet now gone as an old blond real estate agent chosen to represent Ms. America tells him to stay asleep and forget his past.

"As war becomes dishonored and its nobility called into question those honorable men who recognize the sanctity of blood will become excluded from the dance, which is the warrior's right, and thereby the dance will become a false dance and its dancers false dancers."[7]

Bateman calls his secretary one more time as he cries out for help, pleading with her to deny him of the identity his society has prescribed to him. She looks through his journals as his final witness.

Returning to the office for the final time in the movie,

Bateman sits down with his boys again as one of them makes a call with the massive cellular phones of the 1980s that Bateman held the night after he killed one of the many women of the movie. He looks around in terror to question not if he is going to prison, but if anyone can recognize how insane he is. One last jab to Japanese manufacturing is made as Bateman finds out that his lawyer who he confessed to over the phone needed to cover up Bateman's murders because he himself was covering up his own set of sins. Realizing the collective lie he is living in, Bateman looks around his office in horrific acceptance as he wonders of the collective lies of the men in the room. Sitting down alongside his friend looking at Ronald Reagan lie about the Iran-Contra affair over the television that sits hung in the corner of the room like one in a prison, Bateman becomes one of the boys, as he mutters to himself *inside doesn't matter* when his friend Bryce brings up how Reagan's public image that represents the "sincerity" of the American people never reflects the sincerity of their war machine. Bateman, now seeing himself reflected in the people around him, simply adopts the vacuity of war itself as his personality rather than letting the concept, or supposed morality of it, drive him insane. Much like the Judge in <u>Blood Meridian</u>, or the God of the old testament, Bateman becomes war itself as he loses the naivete of having believed he was not a part of it. He loses his private self to his public self, as to try to distinguish between them becomes meaningless. The question then becomes, as war becomes ignoble, if the dance was false before Bateman joined it, and recognized the meaninglessness of the gesture, or after, when the gesture becomes meaningless altogether.

"Every age has its own divine type of naivete, for the discovery of which other ages may envy it: and how much naivete—adorable, childlike, and boundlessly foolish naivete is involved in this belief of the scholar in his superiority, in the good conscience of his tolerance, in the unsuspecting, simple certainty with which his instinct treats the religious man as a lower and less valuable type, beyond, before, and ABOVE which he himself has developed—he, the little arrogant dwarf and mob-man, the sedulously alert, head-and-hand drudge of "ideas,"

9

of "modern ideas"!"[8]

-Nietzsche

Nostalgia can then be said to be the moment in which the blood of the age must be reunited with the blood of the past, the moment in which the sincerity of the American people is akin to the violence of childbirth itself. The characters of Alan Moore's <u>Watchmen</u> turn to nostalgia, after all, because they are as trapped as Bateman was, trapped to looking into the past to be reminded that there is no present. For if there is one emotion man is bound and enslaved to that the Greeks could not personify, it was Nostalgia herself, the allure of victory trapped in the sensuality of a past already gone, but endlessly in the present future. She is the ultimate allure for war, the spiritual requirement all men have died and fought for.

"War. War never changes."[9]

Antithetical to *American Psycho* is the now out of favor *Sex in the City*. Serving as the female counterpart to *South Park*, *Sex in the City* masterfully crafts storylines about women's private sex lives and how it affects them in public interactions. If *American Psycho* depicts the psyche of a man tormented by psychosexual symbols of free sex in a society where women are adored despite their paid labor, *Sex in the City* is a celebration of the wars fought to ensure women could be sex symbols and be paid for their labor. Both written by gay men, *Sex in the City* depicts what would happen if a gay man had, instead of trying to be a straight man like he does in *American Psycho*, tried to be a straight woman in capitalist New York City instead. Mastering the writing advice *South Park* creators gave to students at NYU, *Sex in the City* follows these principles:

"We found this really simple rule that maybe you guys have all heard before, but it took us a long time to learn it. We can take these beats, which are basically the beats of your outline, and if the words 'and then', belong between those beats, you're fucked. [...]

What should happen between every beat that you've written down is either the word 'therefore' or 'but'."[10]

"Therefore" and "but" can also be interchanged for an affirmation, and a contradiction, respectively. Dostoevsky is a master of this - each sentence in his novels is an affirmation, and contradiction, of the sentence and information that came before it. A clever visual metaphor for this can be seen when comparing the manga panels of mangakas Akira Toriyama, creator of <u>Dragonball</u>, and Junji Itou, creator of <u>Uzumaki</u>. In his earlier works, Toriyama lacked the finesse to create full masterpieces and best sellers of shonen manga such as Dragonball, but still had the technical skill to create fun, playful panels and characters.

In this page[11], Toriyama, despite mastering character design, chibi cars, and robots, doesn't create meaningful tension as Itou later does. Read right to left, the large "VRRATATAT!" at the top of the page draws you to it, breaking the natural tension of the action between the two panels instead of adding to it. In addition, the driver's gaze draws him to the middle of the next panel between the car and the plane rather than to the plane as it would naturally read during a real life sequence of events. It is more "and then" than "but" and "therefore". Compare this to Itou's work in <u>Uzumaki</u>:

In these two pages[12], read right to left, as done in all manga, the action begins with the tension on the girl's face. Her gaze leads the readers down past her nose onto her boyfriend's head, who then with his gaze, leads the reader right towards the swingset where she is sitting and where he can be seen clutching the swingset chains tightly. Backs turned, they represent solitude to the reader as Itou depicts the town in the background in contrast to his two characters - he constantly feeds the reader information, even building the tension of the swingset using the tree leaves in the previous panel. From here, the reader is drawn naturally back down to the next panel as he follows the angle of the swingset's structure, affirming, doing a "therefore", while adding a "but" afterwards with the male character's gaze, introducing the tension of the story, the need to leave town, as the center of the page, while still keeping in line with the expression of the boyfriend from the top right panel. On the bottom panels, a "therefore" is used not only through text, but the girl's expression as well - she is facing towards her boyfriend on the next page who is facing her on its first panel so as to not break continuity between the couple. The scene's background guides readers along the scene structure as even the "WHOOO" sound effect lies parallel to the boyfriend's neck in the panel sequentially before the siren sounds. In all cases, a "therefore" leads into a "but" almost simultaneously, keeping the reader constantly engaged with the structure of the story through dialogue as well as picture structure.

Sex in the City functions similarly: every twist in the character's love life is met with an unexpected "but" or "therefore" that is reflected in their city lifestyle as New York becomes the backdrop by which characters experience love and romance in their public and private spheres. Each of the four women in the show have, in their public lives, as seen through their shared lunches, a persona that plays into their private love life, assuming, of course, that their time with their friends is their public self, and their time with their lovers is their private self. Perhaps it is this assumption that has made the show more unpopular with women over time. Samantha, for example, is a diva who "has sex like a man", i.e. has easy sex for feelings of power. In public, she is openly flirty with men that she sees as possible for her to have her way with; in private, these men are often hiding secrets that make the power they have unattractive or impossible to access for her. The other women in the show face similar dilemmas: in public, the men they meet are always full of the promises of hopeful romances they wish to meet, but in private, the men all fail in one way or another to get over their mommy issues. The show's women always have their romances end in tragedy as none of the women finally get their way, but are sex symbols and desirable nevertheless because they still have professional, high end jobs that make ends meet in Manhattan of all places. It is in this way that the women of show are still seen as *men*, because things go their way, and they are given access to the power in society women are deprived of: that of the autonomy, and of the fruit, of their own body.

The women of *Sex and the City*'s spiritual successor, Lena Dunham's *Girls,* live in the shadow of their feminist, sexually liberated 90s New York counterparts. Unlike the women of *Sex and the City*, the women of *Girls* have, in part due to their unattractiveness, no access to their bodies whatsoever; instead, the women only have access to allow others to access their bodies. Mr. Big, *Sex in the City*'s walking phallic symbol and an expression of the male psyche, is shown in contrast to the woman as more decisive, always seen with a cigar the same way Patrick Bateman was in *American Psycho*. *Girls* does something quite the opposite - women and men in power are shown as gatekeepers to Hannah's, the show's protagonist, life. Both women and men fulfill the service of the patriarchy as the women in power in the show of the era of feminists depicted in *Sex in the City* are either non-existent or have betrayed Hannah and her friends. In this absence, the women of *Girls* are left to cope with the men around them granted access to meager capital through remedial jobs, unlike Mr. Big or the men of *Sex in the City*. Adam, the closest thing Hannah has to a husband, has awkward, uncomfortable sex with her, reflective of the kind of immoral sex a porn deprived generation could not imagine. Sex between men and women is depicted solely through this lens and completely without any kind of phallic symbolism or male gaze from the women's part - much like Manet's *Olympia*, the hatred men in real life have of Dunham is in depicting sex in such a raw manner where women's bodies have no role in providing pleasure for the male viewer. It as feminist, and as uncomfortable, as our society is willing to let us experience sex through the visual medium at once.

Filled with millennial weirdness, the show also uses black and Hispanic people living in the ghetto as moral footballs that can be passed around when necessary to show how much Lena Dunham cares about minorities. *Sex in the City* foregoes this altogether, simply focusing on witty showwriting in a show featuring rich white women. While both shows do have semblances of female biology, the misattribution of biology only to *Girls* does not stem from biology, but from its depictions of the reality of sex for women of the millennial era: one in which women are still expected to do the heavy lifting of appeasing, and taking care of, the male ego, while simultaneously live aloofly to the powerlessness of the men around them and in subjugation to the men and women that came before them.

If there is one show that displays the dichotomy between the public and the private, while at the same time, displaying both men and women accurately but equally, I would give the title to the cult classic web series *The Guild*. Premiering 17 years ago in 2007, the internet was then still weird and Americans had not yet become so uncomfortable with their own sexualities that the only aspect of it left was hypersexualized black OnlyFans models on twitter. Stuck between her non existent public persona, her private life, and her public online persona in *World of Warcraft*, femcel Cyd played by Felicia Day begins the show with her therapist breaking up with her as the blending of her private and public life fades away into her third private public space, that of her virtual video game world. It is in many ways the opposite of the struggles of the women on *The Kardashians*, where their public persona is created through a false blend of their private and public selves. Unable to cope with the struggles of modernity, Cyd's therapist tells her to quit the game and get a life or give up on therapy, the old ways of dealing with the public and private dichotomy of American life falling to the wayside. Zaboo, a part of the online guild clan she games with, shows up at her doorstep at the same time as he tries to break away from his overbearing mother while trying to win Cyd's heart over. Bladezz, the guild troll and disgusting teenager who makes hypersexual jokes at women's expense to make up for his own soft sides he is trying to hide, is my spirit animal. Amongst the rest of the cast are men and women with failed private lives who escape into games as an out of their public ones. Cyd, trying to embrace the real world, convinces her and her guild friends to meet up irl while at the same time trying to figure out what to do about Zaboo showing up to her house uninvited - despite being a creep, he is still her friend, and is never emasculated completely for his social illiteracy.

The beauty of the show, and its honest depictions of both online and real world masculinity and femininity, comes from this: that unlike today, where we are so obsessed with out private selves our public ones must be perfect to match them, the characters of *The Guild* are disgusting because we see them in private, and they learned to cope in the real world by retreating into *World of Warcraft*. They are not lesser than us for their disgusting traits; we are lesser than them despite them. I am as desperately attracted to Felicia Day today as when I was 14 and introduced myself to the show online; much like the characters on the show, men and women today are still as depravedly irresponsible and judgemental in our private lives as the guild members were. Beginning in season 2, the show finally begins not when the "real" world accepts them as they create a public persona for themselves akin to their virtual video game ones, but rather when they decide to, as in the video game version of themselves, upgrade their private life in order to accommodate their public ones. Our social media selves, after all, are no different than the video game characters the guild members created for themselves. They are simply reflections of the levels we have put in in order to dive into the virtual world of social media as we choose to believe those are our real selves to hide from our private lives. So despite it being seen as manly to play video games, what could be more feminine, as it happens to Cyd, than being blamed by the men and women in your vicinity, as it happens to her in the show, for having your friend show up to your door, unannounced, proclaim his love for you, and then force his way into your home, only to have his mother call you a whore for stealing him from her? After all, the cardboard box that held my comic books only became a symbol of nerd masculinity when it became a vessel for it.

I RESPECTED SAM HYDE UNTIL I FOUND OUT HE LIKES PHILLIP K. DICK

I began to question the role of art school in 21st century America most prominently in my junior and senior year of college when I began watching and reading Brad Troemel's work while playing *Fallout: New Vegas* before my art classes at University of California San Diego. Despite being an architectural marvel, the school became a hub for artless, Christianized ABGs and other Asian American groups who have very little in the ways of culture whatsoever. Despite having families from Asia, they were only ever united by anime and 88 Rising, rarely ever the Angkor Wat or Hokusai paintings. I questioned why I was being taught Duchamp over Matt Furie's <u>Boys Club</u>, considering the most important image of the 21st century is most likely that of a poorly drawn cartoon frog, or why all the women in my class were parodies of some outdated New York mode and style of social justice Andy Warhol invented alongside Basquiat in the late 1980s. Friends and students were quickly offended when I told them I did not like the aforementioned painter, as if their entire coolness factor was destroyed when I said I preferred graffiti writers over Basquiat himself. We were all so depressed after the pandemic it was hard to make any meaning out of anything; the mere idea of college after virtual learning seemed tantamount to nothing at all. Left uninspired by the mindless dread of a generation succumbing to fear as more and more we hid away from society to protect ourselves, I turned to *Fallout: New Vegas* only to find out my art classes were more obscene than it. During one, a professor pointed to his powerpoint slide that would have earned me a C+ during high school, so poorly put together and designed it like seeing a child trying to fit in the letters from a Campbell's alphabet soup can into the grids of a waffle, that I questioned just why I should study his preferred art pieces over *Fallout: New Vegas*. Looking like the failed idea project of someone too crazy to work on the original *System Shock*, my professor lectured to us as to how we were uncultured for not admiring or knowing the work of an artist's whose name I forget that hooked up a man's muscles to electric signal emitters that, using the most primitive forms of internet connection, allowed users across the world to shock his muscles into movement in some grotesque display of the interconnectivity of the human race. Laughing to myself, I sat in my class as no one even questioned or mocked my professor's taste, questioning as to exactly why I was, instead of speaking about the beauty of games like *Fallout*, discussing what seemed to be an art piece a character from the *Fallout* series would have invented. Before, he had shown the world's first interactive camera displays, where cameras in LA and New York were connected through television screens for the first time. All I could do was laugh and think about all the Indian guys masturbating my friends and I saw on Omegle before the website was shut down.

Gaming culture itself, like the rest of the internet, has seemingly shut down in its own ways. Once decidedly male and "white" coded, video games have become politicized beyond repair as streamers such as Sneako can barely handle seeing a woman in COD games. What was once a subculture with core games such as *Fallout 3*, *TF2*, and other such games on the r/gaming banner has been replaced by the politically divisive r/gamingcirclejerk, which is proudly pro-trans and inclusive despite literally being named after an activity that describes men getting together and masturbating in a circle to see who can ejaculate first. Women, who were "excluded" from gaming through marketing after the video game crash of 1983[13], are slowly being "introduced" into the subculture through marketing schemes and tactics as the streamers and celebrities that started playing video games made women compete for appeal in the sexual marketplace through vapid references to video games only the normie basic streamers have deemed culturally appropriate. Gamers, however, are not much better; they still spend thousands of hours playing *League of Legends*. It is these same politically correct gamers and the women who are suddenly interested in playing them that seem to believe in the necessity of politically correct video games, despite every major game studio having massive sexual harassment and assault allegations. My least favorite of these has to be *Red Dead Redemption II*, where the second mission has the player walk alongside the gang's black cowboy so that the player can be reminded that "he's one of the good ones", despite the game taking place in the American Wild West of the 1800s. Forced to protect the nobility of Native Americans despite, if being historically accurate as internet "conservatives" claim to want, the multi-racial gang in the game would have spent their time scalping Indians instead of killing white Catholics and white police officers, there is no one else left in the United States that the public feels comfortable killing. Much like the American art institution, so too have games gone the way of foregoing experience for identity and morality, for even the best "white" games and artists of previous generations had more to give to the world than the best BIPOC artists of today. White male gamers, now not the "target" audience, have to put up with shitty games like Valorant and Avowed alongside their non white counterparts like myself as both sides look back to games like *Fallout: New Vegas*, its critique of war, American culture, and fascism, all at once, while at the same time, much like myself in my art class, questioning just who the fuck gave my white professor a pass.

This is to say less of the fake outrage generated online when games such as *Battlefield 1* include women and black people in their games as playable characters, despite those being role playing fantasies like *Fallout* and not "historically accurate" games like *Red Dead Redemption II*. As one user on 4chan summarized, whose post has been lost to time and so I am unable to quote, it is incredible that 10 years ago, when *Assassin's Creed III* came out, a Native American assassin was the pinnacle of badassery, but today, to think to do so would be unimaginable. I have a feeling this has something to do with BLM riots and the vapid women entering the gaming space, but the comment about women was always said about gamers, and it is college professors that are supposed to exploit young people's college debts to do sociology research about the effect race riots in America had on video game subculture, not me.

That being said, it is important to at least *try* and include video games in the art roundtable, even if older white men, their whores who collectively refer to themselves as "artists", and their followers, sneer and look down upon the hordes of American college students who only became artists because of video games in the first place. Apart from the art itself, which like in all mediums, follows the law of scale and color theory, games differ in their ability to create tone and mood through player experiences that exploit the pleasure-pain principle. Build up tension, then release it all in one go, as Mashiro Sakurai explained in his video game lecture series.[14] Much like any film building emotional or dramatic tension through cinematography, so too must games build and then release tension to drive a sense of fun, and advance the plot, of their game's story. Tone and mood are then delivered by the way the game balances its risk and reward system with the larger emotional and story beats it wishes to drive home. An action horror game like *Resident Evil 4* will require its player to manage the strategy and rhythm of resource management that gives it the fear and suspense-inducing tension of a horror game. At the same time, *Resident Evil 4* must deliver on the action half of its gameplay, meaning arcade-like fun and action sequences are delivered throughout the game as opposed to games like *Call of Duty* where single player fun is only relegated to shootouts, on behalf of the game's action only tone. *Five Nights at Freddy's*, on the other hand, which is completely horror based, restricts the player's movement to a single room altogether. In doing so, it removes freedom of movement, and in turn, control, from the player, to induce a suspenseful tone of gameplay that induces shrill horror moods in the game's atmosphere.

Platformers induce tone to invoke moods of fun and exploration through geometry and freedom of movement as well, but on completely different levels. In platformers, height and scale are the bread and butter of design - they are the restrictions by which a designer forms the language of his player's exploration, and of how they relate their character, and its freedom, to the confines of the world designed for it. When comparing an instant failure like *Balan Wonderworld* with an instant classic like *Super Mario Odyssey*, it becomes clear at a glance just how wrong Balan's developers were in comparison to Mario's. In the Mario game, Mario's cartoon proportions are proportioned to the cartoon world around him. Heights and platforms are drawn out to different heights to give players a sensation of movement unique in each jump and micro platforming puzzle spread out throughout Mario's world - he is never static, and the level design around him, along with its color palette, reflects this. In *Balan Wonderworld*, the player's character is always half the height of every block in the world - he is restricted, even in 3D space, from fully capturing the gravity and animation of his jump height that changes with the smallest dynamic pressings of the buttons that control Mario.

Corn Kidz 64, a recent indie venture that is necessary of having its creator's vision be crowdfunded, takes the aspect of platforming storytelling to another level. In its owl level, each dynamic platforming puzzle unlocks not only the next platforming challenge, but also expands on the world that came before it. Dynamic springs that shoot out of the player's head become bouncing items as the player learns that by flipping into a reverse world he can turn the music box that was left improperly set up the right way, facilitating access into the boss' dungeon. Fulfilling its own prophecy, the game expands on its own worldbuilding through platforming challenges rather than be restricted by them - a masterclass in level and game design.

Apart from this, *Corn Kidz 64* leaves the player with two more levels apart from the tutorial one, both towers with platforming challenges that increase with difficulty as the player climbs it. In either case, the worldbuilding of the owl level is lost, depicting the challenge of creating purely platforming based games: in the tower without checkpoints, anxiety and strategy are intertwined as difficulty is equated with gaming endurance. Too many checkpoints, as in the tower with platforming puzzles but no anxiety, and the tension of the game becomes unfulfilling when released. In all three cases, however, *Corn Kidz 64* is a necessary case study for the different progressions and diversity found in 3D platformers, displaying the strengths necessary for each type of level.

This is in complete contrast to the cinematic, realism based physics engines associated with Sony or Xbox consoles. On those platforms, player movement is often restricted to give the feeling of realism or create cinematic tension, that while creating tone through simulating real life physics, also restricts the ability of the player to have authentic in-game experiences as caused by the freedom of a cartoon platformer's physics engine. The color of cartoon-like game design is also removed - the addition of realism often takes away from the ability to create a color palette designed to evoke mood or emotion, as leaf graphics take precedence of world building through artistic vision.

Scale and size are at the heart of inspiration for the majority of games, as evidenced by the level design and strategic gameplay of a game like *F-Zero GX*. The game itself is no different than a third person car racing minigame seen in *Yakuza* games where the player, inside the video game, designs and assembles a custom model car for the in-game race tracks. In *F-Zero GX*, however, the camera is scaled in and the player controls the car directly from the third person. Race tracks are re-designed and textured to give the player the sensation of going 700 km/hr without ever realistically reaching that speed as in-game personalities are developed perfectly for mass marketing and children's toys. Much like the rest of the 90s Japan gaming toy and gaming world, cars are customizable to develop different strategies against opponents like trading card decks in *Yu-Gi-Oh!* and other media franchises did. *F-Zero GX*, a SEGA developed game, also marks the end of an era in Japanese game design where arcades where the foundation for gameplay, and one in the world of video game design as a whole: tabletop rpgs and other physical gameplay experiences,

such as the bug fighting that inspired pokemon[15], no longer serve as the inspiration for video games. Instead, much in the same way literature stopped serving as the foundation of all art, so too did video games simply begin to only look at other video games for inspiration.

WHITE WOMEN ARE STILL RETARDED

The first time I was annoyed at the black best friend stereotype was when I was in college, watching a tv show with a friend I was awfully too mean with, Elmar. *iCarly*, a show from our youth that became popular once girls our age repurposed it for nostalgic reasons as they tried to display some false cultural knowledge as they decided liking it would be cool again, had gotten a reboot. *iCarly* was a show made by now accused foot fetishist/pedophile Dan Scheineder. He may or may not be a pedophile for associating with children all the time but certainly made too many foot and hobo jokes for me, even as a child, to wonder why exactly the people who made *iCarly* thought the word hobo was so funny. Watching *iCarly* after I had moved back from the United States to Venezuela for the first time was the moment in which I realized that the actors in Spanish dubs were not actually speaking Spanish, and that someone else was doing it for them.

The new show was awkward and unfunny in a way perfect for millennials but meaningless for anyone interested in rotting their brain through constant tv flashing *with substance*. This is probably a good time to quote John Waters but I am not cool or gay enough to do so. The reboot was about as inoffensive as you could get, for an American audience, unless you are me, and are trying to, as a light skin Venezuelan in the United States, explain to your vaguely ethnic Middle Eastern American nerd friend why black best friends characters in American media bother you so much. Filled with scenes of Miranda Cosgrove, Carly, being taught "black" slang by her black best friend, Harper, I tried to explain to Elmar why this angered me so much and as to why you gotta let black Americans have some stuff for themselves. Despite having appropriated, especially today, fashion and day to day wear from black Americans, and particularly Hip Hop associated fashion, the only people who respect anyone for such fashion are black Americans without access to it. The only people, after all, that seem to care about someone wearing Supreme today are the few who are poor but simultaneously hard working enough to see it as a status symbol.

The black best friend trope was eventually created into a full movie called *One of Them Days* starring Keke Palmer and SZA. My first time ever hearing about Palmer was from these two gay middle eastern "white" liberals from my high school and the occasional tik tok sound - I was too old to know her as a Nickelodeon star. Playing a waitress from the ghetto in the film, Palmer was much too professional, and too groomed as a child, to fit the role well. Having forgotten it was a blackface movie where the "racial" question of the Aunt Jemima dynamic is foregone by having both characters be black, I invited my mom to go watch it with me at the finer Superlux half an hour from our suburb-town in Massachusetts. When we arrived, I was surprised to see how rundown the Superlux had gotten - a black woman in a tracksuit looking as if she had just finished a black and mild walked out of one of the theatres with her two kids as uncleaned popcorn crunched on carpeted flooring in front of empty theatres. Needless to say, my mom, despite liking finer things, was Venezuelan enough to enjoy our time there.

The movie itself was anything less than strange - its tone flowed in between that of a children's cartoon and a movie as it tried to figure out for itself what it wanted to be. Was it a buddy cop action movie? No. Was it about the struggles of the ghetto? Not exactly - they were poor, but not poor enough for, as someone from the third world, for me to relate to. They were still decidedly American, the metaphors for gentrification still unable to address the reality of America's ghettos - when I watched the trailer a second time, I was hopeful to see an American story of a waitress trying to find love or romance. Most of all, however, was the jarring reality that many of the people in the room, both black and white, were laughing at the *idea* of a person speaking like what they think black/ghetto people sound like. The movie would constantly break in tone to do this "blaccent", despite never actually engaging with African American English the way, for example, DJ Daniel does, or depicting racial/class divides the way *The Vince Staples* show does. Americans still seem to misunderstand that saying "hood" stuff has very little to do with the rhythm or vernacular of black American English, and the film's tone suffered because of it - it was near impossible to differentiate if the film was trying to be "black" for "comedic" purposes and breaking its tone because of it or if that tone was created because immaturity is the only way the black experience in America could be depicted. Palmer would go onto winning a NAACP image award for her performance despite doing nothing for black people in a year where Denzel Washington produced an August Wilson play for Netflix. The awards, hosted in Hollywood, had their clips posted on the BET youtube page underneath a podcast show called "For the Fellas" where black men hide their extramarital affairs under the guise of "black excellence". One of the men on the podcast complained about not being able to go out every weekend because of his work life, which is hardly what I would consider a "black" experience. The majority of black Hollywood, it seems, has resorted to simply celebrating themselves in the name of "representation" rather than making meaningful art.

Coming home that night, I walked in on my mom in my family's TV room as she watched *Little*, a 2019 film starring Issa Rae. Rae is somewhat of a black darling in America today, able to fill American millennial generational values while saying very little about black America at all - I mostly hate her for being a walking stereotype of condescending millennial values that put vapidly political work such as her own over better art pieces of any genre. *Little* is no better, so laughably bad I'm surprised it was produced. The film stars a successful black woman, unloved and seen as a bitch for the strength she is required of by her society to be have in order to be successful. Cursed to be in a child's body, the film is similarly castrated as *One of Them Days* was, forced into immaturity through tone cuts with "black" phrases cut in as the reality of the black woman's life in the movie is covered up through toxic positivity. Rather than reconcile with the fact that her success meant only a young man could love her, *Little* tries to end on a happy ending rather than confront the reality of a successful black woman's solitude. There is, of course, a difference between romanticizing the struggle and simply showing it; for the true black story of *One of Them Days* is not in the struggle that Palmer plays in the film, but rather that Palmer's acting skills had to be pushed aside into an immature script for children and millennials still unable to reconcile with the tension, and reality, finally seen when Palmer explodes at SZA as she realizes how horrible of a friend she is.

"It is only in his music, which Americans are to admire because a protective sentimentality limits their understanding of it, that the Negro in America has been able to tell his story. It is a story which otherwise has yet to be told and which no American is prepared to hear."[16]

-James Baldwin, "Many Thousands Gone"

While once true, this sentiment holds true today no more. More and more so is his story even less accessible through music as rap music, by now the only relevant form of music in the United States, outside of asexual indie rock for liberals and fake country music for failed cowboys, drifts away from black Americans in order to be sold. In his essay "The Blue Guide", Roland Barthes writes:

"Protestant morality [...] has always functioned as a hybrid compound of the cult of nature and puritanism. (regeneration through clean air, moral ideas at the sight of mountain tops, [...] etc.) [...] For the blue guide, men exist as [...] a mere introduction, they constitute a charming and fanciful decor, meant to surround

the essential part of the country: its collection of monuments. [...] To select only monuments suppresses at one stroke the reality of the land and that of its people, it accounts for nothing of the present, that is, nothing historical, and as a consequence, the monuments themselves become undecipherable, therefore senseless."[17]

Today, black American "culture" is told and experienced in the same way. The only black products that matter are those, that much like the Spanish man in the tourism brochure, have nothing to do with the lived experiences of black Americans, the rhythm nor the dialect - only the clothes, the luxury of the lifestyle lived through Future's songs, and seldom the pain. It is this pain, which is only ever expressed through melody or xanax inspired vocals, that the black man himself is represented, ahistorical and senseless in a culture that purifies him through black excellence and its pimp based, "dandy" aesthetics.

White liberal author and assistant literary professor at Harvard Anna Wilson hopes to do the same to fanfiction. Unable to reconcile with the fact that her retarded erotica from Tumblr has as much of a right to be read in academia as the 4chan posts I quote in my essays, that is to say, very little if not only to make a subtle joke, she nevertheless became famous for a paper of hers titled "Fan fictions and premodern literature: Methods and definitions". In it, she writes:

"Tangled in the roots of Jenkins's poacher metaphor is the premodern past. Both Jenkins (implicitly) and de Certeau (explicitly) compare fans to premodern subjects who evaded, resisted, and occupied the margins of different interpretive authorities and institutional powers. Both connect the commons of fandom to the commons of premodern law, and both, to different degrees, situate their theorized reader in an imaginary, nostalgic premodernity. This association between the communal ownership of stories and the imagined premodern is built into the foundations of fan studies built on Jenkins's work, which itself drew on the self-understanding of the fan communities he studied."[18]

While I wish I could write at the legalistic and literary

capability of Wilson, what is important here is precisely what Wilson is suggesting: that the ability of fanfiction to be read in an academic setting is not based on aesthetic merit alone, as Harold Bloom would suggest, but based on the principles of manifest destiny, of looking to an idyllic, European past, to form an anti-Imperialist, American future, as our founding fathers did. Fanfiction writers "evade and resist" institutional power by "uplifting" marginal voices the same way America's voice was elevated through manifest destiny. So too has black art been relegated to the same moral subjugation; for it is not their stories that are being celebrated, but rather the destiny that was manifested in their name.

DON'T CALL ME WIGGER, NIGHTY

I attended the ICE Girls magazine event through @Las Flaquitas NYC's instagram page. Browsing through their stories, I invited myself to random "black/POC" events throughout that city that while claiming Hip Hop seemed far removed from the gangsterism it produced or was produced from. Doing my best to do a Patrick Bateman impression, except this time by monologuing about Kanye albums, 50 Cent's discography, and why Bad Bunny's album is totally a decolonization process and not simply going to further the gringofication of his culture, I entered into the "art" gallery, if you could even call it that. I'm still sickened by the sheer overwhelming amount of colors I saw in New York that night, the outdated Hip Hop music drowning out the thousands of refugees housed on taxpayer dollars as city police do their best to protect the rights of black Americans to be criminals but illegal immigrants to stay illegal. The day before, during an art class at the New School I enrolled in, a black girl I spoke to could not imagine that Venezuela was a bad place to live, despite my patriotism about it. They had to lie to her about the quality of her life, and in turn, accepting the lie, she had no choice but to believe the same lie about my country. The fear of Venezuelans not being morally pure, and from a morally pure land, overshadowed the city with guilt weeks before the second election of Donald Trump. Americans in the Northeast were unable to speak about the election beforehand. They needed Trump as much as they needed him to deport the migrants; they wanted them deported, but they needed Trump to do it so they could reassure themselves of their own corrupt morality in the process. His towers, impossible to see from the venue of the night, still stood proudly in New York City, a city once synonymous with his life and image, that, in trying to corrupt him, merely corrupted themselves in the process.

I misattributed the constant violence of New York City that targets any outsiders to their world as some kind of racism thrown my way, not yet realizing I was soon to become part of the tireless violence of the city itself. I masqueraded away my silence through sarcasm, laughing as I hoped at once to be part of the crowd, but knowing how hopelessly awful doing so would be. Hip Hop without Venezuelan migrants would be to have no Hip Hop at all. I knew how awful the song choice of the DJs was set to be. Even in New York City Pop Smoke does not play anymore. After I put up one of my posters I made for an art class in the venue, a woman took it down and looked at me in disgust. I imagined myself as a shinobi from Naruto carrying a magic scroll as I did so; they needed an artist but were sorely lacking in that department, instead celebrating their Hennessy brand sponsorships instead. The streets of New York City seldom see the blood of rappers shed in today's age, instead running sick with the liquor of Hip Hop lifestyle merchandising that not even the lowest of homeless could hope to cup in their hands and drink for vigor like Greek ambrosia. On a later day in New York, a van filled with black entertainers in mink coats and gold chains opened its doors for hot dogs on a street corner stand. A homeless black woman asked me for help buying one, and when I told her to ask the celebrities on the corner, she told me that the rich never help.

The event itself was at a strange confluence of Protestant values and American Hip Hop aesthetics that while claiming to be black failed in truly being anything at all. *Morenas* dressed in bikinis turned softcore porn into a New Balance magazine fad as their white power sponsor helped them celebrate and make icons out of themselves through shooting each one in the image of their favorite magazine ads throughout American history. Filled with body positivity, the lack of negativity in the magazine seemingly removed any eroticism from it as, much like the new SKIMS push up bras with false nipples to poke through sheer tops, the women in the magazine are sold as catering to the "female gaze". Hypersexualized for the sake of other women, the ICE girls ask men not to stare or catcall them as they trap themselves in the images of women men made to sell their beauty back to them; much like the allusions to Iceberg Slim's <u>Pimp</u>, ICE girls seem to forget just who beat who in Slim's world. Whores, after all, are whores not because they sell their bodies, but because after being beat, they thank their pimps for the medicine he bought for them so they could forget their pain.

Despite most likely being the "whitest", and by far, of the lightest skin there, I have little doubt that I was the only participant of the ritual, that like the false sneers against men of the women in the magazine, had read any of Iceberg Slim's works. Rather than celebrate "blackness", they celebrated the American sneaker company that allowed them to make softcore porn of themselves. Turned into protestant monuments, much like DEI themselves, and in a charge of irony, the women of the magazine, much like the women in Drake's "Nice for What" music video, represent Christian morality as a whole. So pure, so white is our society, so Christian, that even a black woman, the "lowest" of all women in the mythological New York American caste system, can hypersexualize herself for a sneaker ad without needing to worry about the male gaze or be labeled impure in the process. Don't worry about the women being trafficked in New York City tonight, tempts the girl on the back of the magazine holding up her ass with allure in her gaze. Instead, call *Hielo Express*, 1-800-ICE-GIRL, as the cholas in Los Angeles they took inspiration from get written out of New York's urban life. The state of women in New York has hardly changed after all this time; the only monument left to protect them being the Trump tower, which provides shade for Russian prostitutes at nighttime.

"*The true raison d'être of the Negro press can be found in the letters-to-the-editor sections, where the truth about life among the rejected can be seen in print. It is the terrible dilemma of the Negro press that, having no other model, it models itself on the white press, attempting to emulate the same effortless, sophisticated tone—a tone its subject matter renders utterly unconvincing. It is simply impossible not to sing the blues, audibly or not, when the lives lived by Negroes are so inescapably harsh and stunted. It is not the Negro press that is at fault: whatever contradictions, inanities, and political infantilism can be charged to it can be charged equally to the American press at large. It is a black man's newspaper straining for recognition and a foothold in the white man's world. Matters are not helped in the least by the fact that the white man's world, intellectually, morally, and spiritually, has the meaningless ring of a hollow drum and the odor of slow death. Within the body of the Negro press all the wars and falsehoods, all the decay and dislocation and struggle of our society are seen in relief."[19]*

ICE MAG Issue 1, October 2024, page unknown

In the case of the DEI morality and its backlash, one must look no further than Kai Cenat to understand how Americans construct morality. Whether it be the "left" saying that black Americans and their mistreatment is the source of the country's immorality, or the "right" saying that black Americans are immoral in nature and must be "dealt" with, the morality of the country continues to be wrapped up inside, and constructed by, the idea of the black man in the collective subconscious. This is what DMX meant when he said:

"I mean, I guess.... What, they gon' give a dog a bone? There you go. Ooh, we have a Black president now. They should've done that shit a long time ago, we wouldn't be in the fuckin' position we in now. With world war coming up right now. They done fucked this shit up then give it to the Black people, "Here you take it. Take my mess."[20]

in his infamous interview where he first found out about Barack Obama running for president. Kai Cenat, and by that virtue, clothing "brands" such as Who Decides War? are extensions of the same moral virtues. While many hate on Kai Cenat for being himself in public and on live streams, what he functionally represents is what Americans and American advertisers have collectively agreed upon being a black man in the country. People can tune into him not just to be reassured of their own coolness, but to be given access to the swagger of a young black man from the Bronx, be given an access to their world, and have their identity created against, or in his image, in the process.

Rather than be a symbol of how far we have come as a country, the brand Who Decides War? shows how deeply racist it continues to be. Its Jewish/Hollywoodist inspired immigrant story repackaged as pro-black anti-American imperialist clothing with protestant, bourgeois worldviews of Caribbean people and culture is nothing but a showcase of how far we have come in engineering advertiser friendly, "pro-black" people so Lexus can sponsor Complex podcasts. Instead of challenging the status quo, it becomes it as their "radical" black aesthetics become far enough away removed from the experience that car companies can sponsor their shows. Advertisers, after all, have agreed that black men killing one another is American friendly, and a part of black culture. Malcolm X, and his perceived antisemitism however, is deemed by advertisers to be neither black culture nor advertiser friendly. This is to say nothing of the quality of either Kai Cenat or Who Decides War? - far from it. Rather, their "coolness" factor exists insofar as the American need of "freedom of speech" be forced upon black Americans as advertisers collectively agree they exist "outside" of the morality of the rest of the country. It is not that black Americans invented high fashion or streetwear, but rather that they invented the ability for it to be sold to a populace ready to be exploited for its high prices - and in turn, sell a "black" identity as a product equivalent to fame in the process. The whole idea of black fashion continues to be made in the image of the black pimp from the streets of Harlem, an idea by now so fascistic, it makes you wonder if these black women even knew what they were signing up to begin with. This is all the worse when one realizes that the majority of the effort in "raising" awareness campaigns contributes to the profits of the social media companies marketing and making money off of posts of black squares on instagram, not the other way around. Black Americans may try to supplant this by claiming Latinos are more immoral and racist than themselves, but it only shoves the debt even further away from the question of who is going to pay back the country's moral debt at all.

I was myself caught in this position when the weekend of the ICE magazine show aligned itself with Halloweekend and an erotic art fair in Bushwick combined. I was attracted, and made aware of, the show through @mobshity's instagram page, a homoerotic man of unknown sexuality famous for his pen dot tattoo fan art of erotic art on t-shirt canvases. He became known to me in part for his recreation of Namio Harukawa illustrations onto t-shirts through his artistic process - mobshity attaches a sharpie to a tattoo gun, replacing the needle with the marker, to make his drawings. The event itself was full of freaks and perverts displaying their own collections of porn as the history and slumlike dredges of New York's past and present came together. Admiring some of the Japanese Shibari novels alongside imported Japanese collector's books of Namio Harukawa drawings, I was surprised as to how doctored their fetish porn was. Rather than simply represent smut, or the perverted desires of man, Japanese erotic imagery were monuments to their corporate culture, monuments of the Japanese corporate man's desire for the subjugation, and immortalization, through erotica, of his women. The women in fetish art, posed and depicted like Greek statues, were not simply decorum of a man's mind, they were each the opulence of the dark underside the corporate world of Japan hid. Harukawa's work existed in contrast to this decorum of the Japanese woman as ornate decoration in their corporate society. If the corporate man reveled in making her an ornate object, Harukawa revealed in showing the Japanese man's reflection back at him. The more he wishes his spouse to be subject to his will, the more he himself becomes a slave to her, becoming her furniture, and her bathtub, in the process.

I turned from here to a Western magazine section. A model from LA was outside dressed like a Moebius character while a black man in a cowboy hat sat across from a white porn collector of his elk outside on the patio. Flipping through the American pornography of the 20th century for inspiration, it was, in contrast to the Japanese variety, smut, lower art meant for the common classes. Unlike the doctored positions of the high Japanese erotica, the crass cartoons and vapid exotification of "oriental" women in these nudie mags, had, as their sex appeal, jugs, unshaven cunts, and the taste and singe of the cigarettes pimps and adult magazine owners smoked in Times Square in the 1970s. A British woman next to me, short and of brown complexion, commented on the magazine I held. Detailing me of her life story, I was surprised to find out she was a dominatrix by the name of Master Liz. We exchanged commentary before she invited me to a beer as I lied to myself in my mind as I tried to rationalize the insanity of her taking her debit card and buying me a drink. Before we continued our way through the show, I spotted a Players magazine with Pam Grier on the cover - there was an ebony showman there showing off Black Tail and other black erotica alongside the aforementioned magazine. A tension spread through the room like tornados through Kansas in vintage black and white color films as I tried to cross the color line.

My new lady friend pulled me aside from the event the moment I touched the black pornographic magazines - doing research later on, I was surprised to see how high quality the music recommendations of black porno mags are. Taking me outside, I was rudely interrupted from my "research" and continued to speak with my new friend. Having ended the show by looking at black porn, the flirting somewhat stopped as she told me she would go back to her apartment, her British accent carrying with it the polite and jovial tone Americans associate with it. Failing to meet her fantasies, she told me of her own life, of the rich Spanish heir she was currently dominating and dating. Struggling to form together a moral standpoint of her possibly taking advantage of this 20 year old's mommy issues, she alleged her family owned an island that hosted prostitutes from around the world. When I told her I was Venezuelan, she said they were beautiful women but lacked work ethic, subtext meaning they were not as kinky as other nationalities, to which I could only nod my head in agreement as I validated what she told me against my experience with *Venezolanas*. She left me her card before leaving me alone to explore the rest of the fair - I questioned how much further I wanted to advance the relationship, thinking of the "brotherhood" (gang) that asked me if I wanted to be initiated into their group I met on the subway in New York City the week before, or the Guyanese-American man that scammed me for $100 after taking me to underground brothel/gambling den in Manhattan. It was my fault for giving him the money, but the anecdote was worth the trip. Nevertheless, all I could think about about her parent's sex island was that of Jeffrey Epstein's own and how the women he trafficked were originally young painters in the New York art world. One of its most celebrated patrons, Epstein, and the world he dominated, has not done much in the way of women's rights since him - young women in New York City art galleries are still, for the most part, glorified slaves in black turtlenecks in front of spiritually devoid paintings. The binary that the non-binary speak of is derived from this: that art is an expression of a man's ego, and phallus, and that women are expected to be submissive to it, regardless of the quality of the art. While New York abstract artists may have freedom of expression, their black and poor seldom have freedom of movement, instead segregated and restricted by the false promise of movement created in the segregation of subway lines and bus routes. Because despite of all that the New York Times and their liberal elite have said about Joe Rogan, they seem to forget he never sexually harassed women on the way to becoming the voice of the American people. Going back into my own Bushwick art gallery once more, I entered the second room of erotica to see men and women coming together to brush over the rape joke cartoons of a bygone era of New York City. The question, after all, was never really one of race, or immigrants, or Jews, or even women, but if living in Manhattan is worth the millions imprisoned in the boroughs around it, for I have seldom seen a rapper that has not regretted the music he made or the lifestyle he promoted.

The rest of the event was tense with the mistrust racialized New Yorkers consistently carry. I finally saw @mobshity and his art in person, pleased by his friendly laid back demeanor. He looked like the main character of a fantasy novel or RPG underneath the lamps he mounted to display the erotica he redrew on t-shirts. I could only think of my father as I wondered if I should buy any, and thought of the decreasing number in my bank account afterwards, deciding to simply shop with my eyes rather than my money. In the back corner of the venue was the gay porn section where a millennial man came to restock on his VHS collection who I asked if he felt that gay porn was gay representation - his response was forgettable, but not the military men he chose to watch have sex with each other on VHS.

Much like the gay culture born out of this perversion, so too was the history and culture of New York City captured through the fair. I eventually caught up and became acquainted with one of the men who had created the smut scene of an older, wiser, and more disgusting New York. Once he and his era of smut had been cleared out, both by online pornography and urban renewal, the Hipster era moved in as gay porn on VHS was replaced by gay erotica artists and their female, tasteful, Japanese erotica enthusiasts. The last step in this process was the girlification of pornography itself, the final step in false feminine liberation, that of white girls getting naked for irony in the 2010s.

The white girls of Vice Magazine, much like the "liberated" white women of the 2010s hipster era, only felt flashing their tits and nudity was a virtue, a Christian value, once the streets of New York City had been cleansed of prostitution, porngraphic theaters, peep shows, and the rape jokes that came along with them, altogether. The only remnants remaining of these ventures were the occasional porno mags in high end magazine shops in SoHo as Harlem re and de gentrified itself at the same time, Billie Holiday's voice permitting. No, much like the women of the negro press, these "feminists" were as "pro-women" as the Negro press was "pro-black". They simply flashed their titties to make up for the void their white fathers left them as they replaced him with a new, equally oppressive white man, one with modern altruistic values of "helping" the negro through song and dance at beer gardens and music festivals instead of at hippie concerts and LSD pop up shows. As stunted as the women of the ICE magazine's "black experience", the femininity of the girls flashing their boobs in Vice magazine were only feminists insofar as the white men around them wanted to see them rebel against *their* fathers, not the patriarchy itself. Caught under the same moral trap the negro press was, these white girls would eventually be eternalized, through "blackness", by the ICE girls, albeit this time in black bodies, as the ICE girls, much like the white feminists of the hipster age, alienated from street porn and prostitution, found themselves "liberated" by the men who published Vice and Players magazine. That night, I met the model from LA at a white hipster party in New York City, only to find out, upon asking its residents, that the majority of white New Yorker Hipsters cannot name a single Miles Davis song, and that all of the Hipster women stopped listening to Lou Reed because every guy they dated who listened to his music had traumatized them in one way or another.

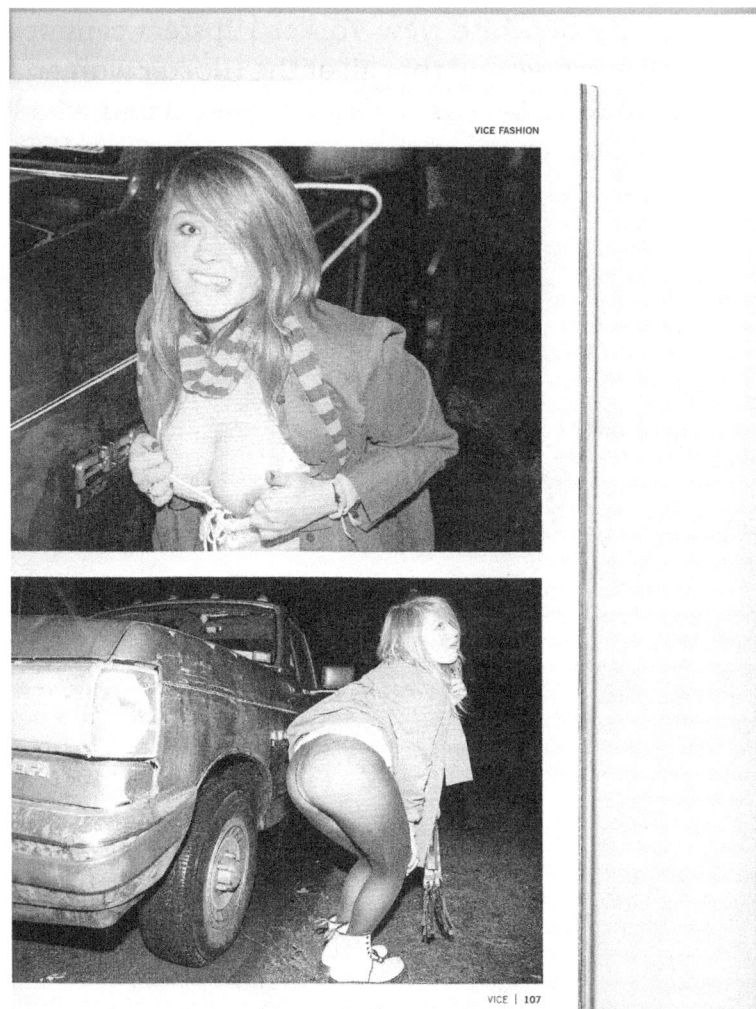

Vice Volume 15, Number 2

By far the strangest thing about the digital era, especially that of the OnlyFans = female liberation generation, is how much men hate pornography, and generally agree on its negative impact on their mental health, and how much women cheer on women who make pornography, despite female adult actresses, for the most part, having their mental health shattered because of it. The question always posed, but never answered by pro sex work enthusiasts, is whether or not a man is pro sex work when he engages in watching pornography or paying for sex. If women can barely afford the WNBA, I doubt they can afford to keep pornhub afloat, leaving men to have, as the representation for women in their early lives, pornstars and girls glazed in bukkake compilations as their first interaction with femininity outside of their mothers and schoolteachers. It is this perversion of our real lives, the bleeding of pornography out of our private lives and into our public ones, that has radically changed the way we view ourselves and the internet. No longer are women asking to stop the hypersexualization of women in video games as Anita Sarkesian was kicked off of the internet for - instead, they look themselves to dress like and emulate the hardcore JRPG bimbos of early 2000s Final Fantasy games for internet profit. The women created for the male gaze in the video games of the 2010s have been appropriated by women themselves as men are left to play emasculated, asexual video games made by and for the pornographic puritan Christian values of the 21st century. For men, this means their gender identity is constructed by contradicting their identity so they can be as close to resembling and being a pornstar as possible - and for women, it means being reassured they can be as attractive, and as hypersexualized, through fashion or otherwise, as an OnlyFans model. If the old adage was "death and taxes", in the digital age, the new constants will be war and pornography. My girlfriend's nudes are immortal when I post them as revenge porn and bitcoin is tax free if done right but only war creates new soyjaks. Porn just so happens to be what I masturbate to to make me forget my mortality.

Ironically enough, this means, in the case of the Catholic

43

church and its new anime mascot, that the art created and born from Japanese Otakus who hypersexualized children in their mothers' basements through lolicon became the symbol of the Catholic church in the digital era. Pathetic. For Kanye West however, this dichotomy has become the center of his new lifestyle and ad promotion, his lust for fame reflected in his desire to make masochistic artistic masterpieces. The perversion of Japanese anime has been forgotten as Americans and the West have blended it into their own style and popular culture as Violet Meyers becomes the de facto face of pornography for men under 15 while Kanye West forces his white wife to make herself a sex symbol by displaying herself publicly nude at the Grammys' red carpet. Fulfilling his life prophecy to the fullest, Kanye displays himself as the ultimate porn auteur as he displays himself as the ultimate sex symbol stomping on the rules of the white world as his new, white, Italian wife becomes the ultimate center of attention for years to come. Forcing her onto the scene against Kim Kardashian and the general public, SKIMS and the rest of Europe has no way to flee from his tirade as he spent years designing and dictating their taste for them. They are now forced, as he has had to, to watch as he screams of their biggest guilt, the holocaust and white supremacy, over videos of white women being whipped by black men next to vintage porn smut pictures of black man on white woman sex while he reflects on his own black holocaust. Racially segregated balloon popping videos become the norm in the background as he does so, black men becoming hypersexual symbols of masculinity while white guys are relegated to the oppressor and the oppressed all at once by the same virtue. This however, does not change the fact that I think Kanye West was talking about black penis sizes in porn when he said that "The size of the Twix gets bigger every year".

White women, after all, still hold some semblance of power in this country, even if they are strangely blamed for a host of its immorality for no apparent reason apart from, like the rest of the country, wanting to be white men themselves, or, more accurately, what they have been lied to about what being a white man is or means. The advertisements targeted at them are strangely gender neutral and asexual as marketing companies try to, in vain, copy rappers like JT who mention "a Birkin" when creating items such as "The Tote Bag"[21]. "High" fashion brands have still yet to catch up with the true shifting demographics of America, still relegating Asian women to gender neutral asexual symbols in Vogue and fashion magazines while Asian women run New York City and Indian men and women are the only ones in the city ever seen together. Pharell Williams decided to exploit his own people by selling their "culture", whatever that even means, to rich Chinese factory owners and their children as Mowalola steals from Andy Warhol to hypersexualize the world as she sees fit, reminding everyone ebony and black were sexual commodities, not cultures, to begin with. FKA Twigs tries to gain a moral high ground on Hollywood executives as Silent Bob lies to the world of Jimmy O. Harris' immorality, despite the fact no one in the United States can even handle going to war, let alone deciding it. The fruits of a failed race war are coming to fruition as even Billie Holiday can sing for New York no more, the only thing left being American puritanism and the pornography it created.

Blood was let at the Oscars in the year of our lord 2025. Moments before the ritual began, women popped out their cleavage as they fought to see who would, in vain, become the next sex symbol and icon for America. None, however, could compete with what Kanye West had done, or was doing with his wife, Bianca Censori. The carpet was tense, empty and devoid of talent as all but failed in trying to live up and recapture an era of Hollywood and celebrity culture now a relic of Y2K fashion and dead tabloid magazine articles. The award ceremony went over fantastically as the sincerity of America came onto full display. Joke after joke made by Conan landed with an audience slowly adapting itself back to normalcy, ushered in by Donald Trump's election, as bombs raged over Gaza in Palestine and "migrants" were held in detention camps across northeastern cities. *Anora* won film of the year as "independent" cinema was celebrated and its director, Sean Baker, glanced over the comments made about celebrating diversity by the man who is now married to Harvey Weinstein's ex-wife. He thanked sex workers and their lives in the process as the new American gender roles as prescribed by Hollywood were rolled out into the public. What more could be said about being a woman in 2025's United States, than being a Russian prostitute, and the good Jewish boys that found a way to love and ennoble them?

R.I.P. Pope Francis
I woke up the day after I wrote this to your death
12/17/1936 - 4/21/2025

BOY POWER, BARBENHEIMER, AND WHY I HATE BOWEN YANG

There has been, strangely enough, a bit of momentum in me drawing me towards the so-called men's activists of today's America. During a conversation that went somewhat viral in some sphere of the internet I do not belong to, Clay Travis, a men's activist and host of OutKick, sat down for a conversation, with amongst others, "sexual culture critic" Magdalene Taylor. The discussion, hosted at UChicago Institute of Politics, was titled "Trad Wives & Alpha Males: Gender Relations in the Blender"[22] as Americans tried to piece together their identity after Donald Trump's election, the most gendered in recent history. Failing to ever actually *define* what a man is, Magdalene, like most women my age, left men and women without an answer as to what women want from a man in 2025. Chosen, because of her "sexually liberated" status as a woman who writes about sex tabloid ready headlines for outlets such as the New York Times, her substack reeks of the kind of vapidity I expect from college educated American feminists - dumb enough to think they are educated for referencing Slavoj Zizek like "one of the boys" as they get propped up to be a spokesperson for women. Her writing, focusing and originating from the racially segregated, white hipster runoff from New York City, poses sex as something fun, vapid, that men can do, and that women should too - despite most men her and my age having little to no sex at all. On a podcast titled "Pleasure-Seeking", Magdalene joins her white friend Camille Sojit Pejcha to be "bad" girls as they talk about sexual trends and other things that are expected to be taboo for women, even if the Greeks knew women enjoyed sex more than men do. Speaking about the recent film *The Substance*, both girls are too stupid to recognize a metaphor when they see one, instead referring to the film as a "fairy tale" instead of a metaphor for womanhood. Frankly, I wonder if the reason she has a job despite her illiteracy is because the men who hire her are so internet illiterate her analysis of internet memes as symptoms of an online psychosexual culture make her seem clever in their eyes. That being said, I've only read her free substack articles - her paywall locked GQ articles seem to have promise, but I could also spend that money on lapdances and learn things from strippers in 5 minutes I will never learn from GQ for years. The question after all, is nor whether or not Magdalene is a white feminist, but if she is enough of a woman to break free from her cultural bubble and zeitgeist to speak to the Hijabis across the street from Hispanic and Asian prostitutes in Queens so that she can find out about femininity and masculinity outside of porno films, Nu Metal, internet trends, and Disney movies.

The aforementioned film *The Substance* tries to do so by breaking free of Hollywood trends, speaking to the ugliness of femininity created and lusted after by those seeking fame in a chauvinistic, pig-like, male producer controlled Hollywood world. Wishing to regain her youth, and in turn, the power and fame her male producers granted for her while she was still in a young body, Demi Moore plays Elisabeth Sparkle, an actress who injects herself with a mysterious "substance" that splits her body into two parts: one young, and one old. Re-incarnated as a young woman, she goes back to the chauvinistic producer that fired her and takes her older version's job as she becomes a starlet in the spotlight once again. As much a critique of the older women in Hollywood's relation to sexuality and beauty of a youthful generation inserting themselves into the same patriarchal system the older women once gained "freedom" and fame inside is the film's religious allegories. Sparkle is a product of the male gaze, but feeds and craves the feeling she gains from being admired; in many ways, in begetting a younger version of herself, she does not yet reincarnate, but, like God giving birth to Jesus, gives birth to a new dilemma: did she create the younger Sparkle through herself, or did her producer create the whole ritual in the first place? Failing to reincarnate, Sparkle abuses the substance and becomes a monstrous version of herself as her old and new selves come together to form a hideous blob that represents the accrued immorality of Hollywood's liberal elite. Dying under three palm trees as Jesus was born under in the Quran, Sparkle's final scene leaves her as nothing but a blob of disheveled human mass on the Hollywood Walk of Fame. Unlike Jesus, she fails to resurrect as God, in this metaphor, herself, fails to be negated on the cross when she tries to take authorship over her younger self's life, forgetting it was she who necessitated her creation so she could feel fulfilled in the first place.

Barbie by Greta Gerwig takes a similar approach to biblical study, posing the question, and answering, "what if God was a woman?" and "what if the garden of Eden was simply girl world all along?" at the exact same time. Starring Margot Robbie as Barbie and Ryan Gosling as Ken, both characters begin in the Barbie world as humans did before Eve ate the apple of knowledge. Sexless and still moving as dolls do, neither character had yet learned the guilt of human reality. Cursed now, to walk the earth, Barbie eventually meets "God", the woman who draws the Barbie character designs, as both characters learn of femininity and masculinity in their own ways. Ken sees the externalization of man through the male gaze while Barbie looks inward in fear to find the peace and calmness to avoid it. In a serene scene, Barbie looks inward for peace and then, seeing an older woman on the bench next to her, shares a moment of shared womanhood as both find desire in one another's serenity. It was, and has been, the only moment in my life, that as a man, being a woman, not seeing a woman, was attractive.

Ken, eventually taking over Barbie world, subjugates the women of it as Issa Rae, originally playing the President of Barbie world, becomes a cocktail beach waitress once Ken takes over. Issa Rae's inclusion in the movie, as president, forces the morality of a nation onto her, forcing her to be the sacrificial lamb for the country's inclusive politics. Despite being about *Barbie*-s, it is difficult not to take Issa Rae's inclusion, in a racialized society such as the American one, with ease. Devising a plan to take Barbie world back from men, the Barbies, having gained the guilt of sexuality, trick the Kens into feeling powerful because Barbie shows interest in them, only to turn the Kens against each other when they strip the power the Kens have away from them. Barbie world returns to normal as women, as they always have, become the generals of the world in the background, and the daughter of Barbie's creator learns to love femininity despite the fact that being a woman means being prescribed to impossible standards of representing all women, but none at all, at the same time. The Kens are left to cope with their egos as Barbie, in the final scene of the movie, leaves the comfort of girl/Barbie world behind the moment she decides to go to her first gynecology appointment. Cruelly witty and beautifully funny, *Barbie* finds a way to portray the immaturity of both genders, and the ignorance unique to them, without offending either. Rather than see it on release day, I watched *Barbie* at a later date. Instead, on the day of the film's premiere, I watched *Oppenheimer* in anarcho capitalist Venezuela with my father as Hijabis in pink headdresses and Venezuelan women, remnants of Venezuela's fourth republic, came together to watch *Barbie* and take instagram pictures in the displays at the Orinokia mall. I spoke about the double premier with my American cousin's from my father's side fiance over dinner months later. She told me, and my sister, that despite disliking the *Barbie* movie, she liked Oppenheimer even less because it "only featured white men". I wondered, if she held such a resentment for them, why she chose to date and wake up next to one every day.

Rather than be films detailing and celebrating the

successes of white men, both *Napoleon* and *Oppenheimer* reflected a shift in a year of feminist movies about men. Rather than glorify their successes, both films tackle the question of male insecurity and its origins the same way *Barbie* did, but with a brutally different tone. The true tension at the heart of *Oppenheimer* is not in the bombs or the scientists that developed it, but rather the egos behind these men that dictated the necessity, and thrill, of the nuclear bomb's invention. Best exemplified in the sex scene between Oppenheimer and his communist girlfriend, his girlfriend knows that to keep him sexually aroused, she must not appease the ego within him that looks for validation through sexual prowess. Instead, she has her read him Bhagavad Gita while she straddles him during sex as he mutters his iconic quote, "I have become death, destroyer of worlds." It is in this scene, that the fate, and the message of Oppenheimer is sealed. Man did not become the destroyer of worlds for peace, nor for carnage, but out of his own ego. *Oppenheimer*, originally in IMAX, cut out during our viewing in Venezuela when the power went out. Despite this, it is the only movie theater in the city. My father and I watched *Napoleon* there later, enamored by the scope of the film's war scenes and the magnitudes Ridley Scott went through to capture the romanticism of war from the perspective of its general. Much like *Oppenheimer*, so too is Scott enamored and inspired by Napoleon Bonaparte's secret or fantastical love life. In the film, Napoleon is depicted as a great general but a failed lover - his love for France, and her common woman, existing in the metaphor for the woman he chooses to love but fails to consistently win over, depicts Napoleon as impotent in private. Man's conquest is, much like in *Oppenheimer*, forever tied to his own sexual appetite and ego - rather than being celebrations of white men's achievements, it is a critique, and a witnessing, of their perceived frail egos. Gone are the everyman victories over Roman emperors and spoiled bratty princes seen in Ridley Scott's *Gladiator*. Instead, it is the generals and leaders themselves who in private showed frailty, not the leaders that were frail in public, that are antagonized. I tried to bring this up to my 63 year old father - he refused to care or listen and instead lectured me about what he thought about both movies.

This all came to a pique when, after the 2025 Oscars, I finally watched *Wicked* with my mother. Confused by its tone, it was filled with the same millennial era, SNL writing that Marvel movies created while at the same time having no discernible demographic whatsoever. Rather than explicitly being about marginal people, the film's use of metaphor meant even a conservative like Ben Shapiro could enjoy the film's message about animals being excluded from the university's fantasy world. Ariana Grande played an innocent, well-to-do princess named Glinda whose stark sentimentality stuck like dissonant notes on parallel cello strings against Cynthia Erevo's Elphaba. Much like Issa Rae in *Barbie*, the film is a direct descendant of the protestant morality of diversity politics that created "DEI" in corporate America. Characters border between asexual and non-existent as Hollywood actors vying for fame come together to make a movie for our inner childs that fails to be for children altogether. If it was, maybe the actors in the movie would not each have been over 30, a symptom of a millennial generation that refuses to grow up or even acknowledge other people in the United States are having kids.

I switched on the first Harry Potter film once I reached *Wicked*'s climax. Inspired by its fantasy setting that tried to rekindle the magic of the Potter world, I was shocked to find out how much we have deteriorated culturally since then. Scenes and moods in the Harry Potter world are each set and stylized like paintings would - unlike the mess of colors and grand dresses of *Wicked* that leave no room for visual information apart from CGI and wardrobe exuberance, Potter's world gives each scene, and bit of dramatic tension, its own style and character. Hagrid's entrance in Potter's life is well edited and uses blues and damp color palettes to convey the moments before Harry enters the world of Hogwarts through the brightly lit train cabins of the Hogwarts Express. Hermione is introduced as the perfect girl archetype, picking up after the bravado and mess of young boys with detail oriented acuity and wit that shows why the Harry Potter series resonated with so many people regardless of gender: it celebrated boys' and girls' achievements at the same time. Women were never relegated to immaturity - Hermione was always seen as more tender, wiser, and detail oriented, than the courageous men of her world, who without Hermione and Ginny they would have not survived. Instead, *Wicked* writes out young men/boys altogether for some pantomime queer/gay fantasy where even Ariana Grande is left depressed by the fact there is not a man, like Hermione could for Ron and Harry, to stand up for her in her world. The death of love, it seems, was pronounced and ushered in by *Wicked*'s inability to foster it. At that moment, I thought back to Clay Travis' conversation with Magdalene Taylor at UChicago and wondered if maybe Travis was right to be confused as to why his son asked him "Why is there no boy power?" at a Target after his son saw a shirt that had, written on it, "girl power". There are no movies featuring young boys becoming men anymore, and in their absence, there are almost no movies about women either; for both masculinity, and femininity, rely on each other: *Oppenheimer* and *Napoleon* are not truly feminist films. If they were, women would not just serve as symbols of men's insecurity, as Hermione was written not to be. And if it is a question of money, why has Hollywood not yet realized that for every male protagonist in their blockbusters of the 20th century, there was always a woman in the movie that women could resonate, and identify, with?

THE UKRAINE WAR AND THE QUESTION OF ARE TRAPS GAY?

"The judge smiled. Men are born for games. Nothing else. Every child knows that play is nobler than work. He knows too that the worth or merit of a game is not inherent in the game itself but rather in the value of that which is put at hazard. Games of chance require a wager to have meaning at all. Games of sport involve the skill and strength of the opponents and the humiliation of defeat and the pride of victory are in themselves sufficient stake because they inhere in the worth of the principals and define them. But trial of chance or trial of worth all games aspire to the condition of war for here that which is wagered swallows up game, player, all.

Suppose two men at cards with nothing to wager save their lives. Who has not heard such a tale? A turn of the card. The whole universe for such a player has labored clanking to this moment which will tell if he is to die at that man's hand or that man at his. What more certain validation of a man's worth could there be? This enhancement of the game to its ultimate state admits no argument concerning the notion of fate. The selection of one man over another is a preference absolute and irrevocable and it is a dull man indeed who could reckon so profound a decision without agency or significance either one. In such games as have for their stake the annihilation of the defeated the decisions are quite clear. This man holding this particular arrangement of cards in his hand is thereby removed from existence. This is the nature of war, whose stake is at once the game and the authority and the justification. Seen so, war is the truest form of divination. It is the testing of one's will and the will of another within that larger will which because it binds them is therefore forced to select. War is the ultimate game because war is at last a forcing of the unity of existence. War is god."[23]

-Cormac McCarth, Blood Meridian

"When I graduated college, I went into the technology industry, the startup industry, because I thought it was one of the last realms of sincerity in the West today - that you could say with a straight face 'I want to build a starship that takes us to Mars', and hire a thousand people who worked 100 hour weeks in total belief, in immersion. [...] What I wanted, entering technology, was that type of ability to devote myself, to throw myself into something. [...] I have a friend who's a very successful fund manager, so he's at the top of the capitalistic pecking order, and the thing he wants most is to go to war. And he isn't, you know, hoping for a small war. He's looking for a war that's gonna threaten North America because he can devote himself existentially to it."

-Johnathan Bi speaking on Nihilism with Robert Pippin, "Nietzsche's Warnings for Modern Man | UChicago's Robert Pippin"[24]

By the time Elon Musk's ascension into stardom through the White House fully materialized, X, formerly known as Twitter, had taken in as refugees from 4chan the majority of its groypers, soyjak posters, and other pseudo white supremacists that despite believing in American ethno nationalism, cannot live without trap hentai. For dumb old people, hentai is internet slang for animated pornography drawn in Japan, and trap is slang for a woman with a penis. Now strangely thrust into the public sphere, the question of the feminine penis that eluded internet philosophers for ages: "are traps gay?", is now a relevant to the fate of America's involvement in geopolitics and possible nuclear war with Russia, and was cleverly summarized in this meme[25] years ago:

"Is it gay to love traps?"

PLATO: "For a man to love traps is not gay by any measure, for traps embody the true form of feminine Beauty, which suffers **no constraint by any earthly gender** but is rather fulfilled in all feminine bodies regardless of their biological origins. For example, one might love and admire a statue of a woman, but we would never call such a person a statue-lover, for it is the form of the Female which is instantiated in the statue that this person admires; likewise with traps. We see that there are some who love traps but despise overly-masculine bodies, and for these people, it is not proper to speak of them as being gay at all, for the nature of gayness, if gayness were to exist, is the love of a gender which is the same as yours. This love is something which has its **timeless origin** in the domain of Forms before it could ever become instantiated in the world of bodies. Therefore, it is not gay to love traps, for one loves not the earthly body of a young boy but a **transcendent Woman-Beauty** that is fundamentally female in nature and completely incorporeal."

ARISTOTLE: "Suppose, for the sake of argument, that traps were **just a species within the genus of women**, just as "tall women" are. This would mean that traps are women, which makes it not gay for a man to love them. However, insofar as traps exist as a distinct species of women, it must be fundamentally gay to love them, for the **differentia** of a trap is the quality of "having been raised as a boy". If one were to be a lover of tall women to the **exclusion** of women of other heights, we would say that this person is a lover of "tallness". Likewise, if one were to love trap-women, to the exclusion of other women, we would say that this person is a lover of the differentiating quality of traps, which is "having been raised as boys," and hence that this person is straight in some ways, but also gay. For it is the **differences** between species from which we derive our definitions. So long as the distinction between trap-women and non-trap-women exists, it must be at least a little gay to love traps. And if it is at least a little bit gay to love traps, then it is certainly gay."

DIOGENES: "Lmao dude, who giveth a fuck about gender-distinctions when you can celebrate the wedding-hymn of your right hand to any person you want?"

Browsing 4chan, as any real philosopher of this age should do, I came across this ten year old discussion, now eternalized by American colleges, while also stumbling across the rebirth of 4chan's politically incorrect forum board, nicknamed /pol/. Basically, anyone on 4chan can post anonymous text and have it be replied to with images attached - threads, collections of an original image/image and text post get deleted periodically after they become old and inactive enough. Similar to twitter but with less individuality focused on "user" experience, 4chan has a bad rep for not being racially segregated enough to make black people as comfortable as they are on Reddit or X. The FBI eventually started posting there and the site was recently hacked and has been inactive for days now, with the possibility of the last 4chan post being a picture of Jack Black from the Minecraft movie tagged "CHICKEN JOCKEY". If so, it would be a poetic ending to the last bastion and hub of somewhat true free speech online, dead alongside LiveLeak to usher in the weakness of the digital age. Browsing the site before its potential and inevitable death, /

pol/, once home to the internet's devout Trump fanatics and the "alt-right", became my source for anything related to the Ukraine war. Strangely enough, once the groypers left, the only people left that posted on /pol/ had an avid passion for politics, especially those related to the Ukraine war. Unlike the rest of the internet, their posts were sincerely devoid of American propaganda or their false morality around the conflict, as if white power, and its wars, means anything during the free trade societies we have come to accept as normal. A direct symptom of this was that, in the daily Ukraine war threads, would always be linked a html text-like file titled:

"DISPOSABLE SOLDIER (diary of a RU mobik) - TOUR 1

(translation courtesy of cofi anon)"[26]

Now that the website is down, I only have access to cofi anon's translation of the soldier's first tour - the rest of the book I translated from Russian to English using ChatGPT. I prefer cofi's version - it has the humanity, and sincerity, GPT's lacks.

"There, [at boot camp], I also tried operating a quadcopter. We called drones "birds." Many were convinced that a drone could see everything happening on the ground and that every other drone was equipped with night vision or thermal imaging. However, this turned out to be completely untrue. The drone I operated was an inexpensive civilian version, and its camera didn't show that much. In reality, against the backdrop of a field or forest, it's indeed possible to see a group of moving people. However, if a person is alone and standing still under a tree, you'll never spot them from a drone! A camouflaged soldier can indeed hide from a drone in vegetation – it works! I pointed the camera at a stationary person from a height of forty meters, but couldn't find him. Of course, a lot depends on the camera quality, the operator's attentiveness, and the density of the vegetation above the person's head. But I realized then that drones aren't all-powerful."[27]

In Dostoevsky's The Gambler, its Russian protagonist attends a German casino to spectate as Europeans gamble hoards of gold won from the spoils of their wars carefully, and stoically, at roulette tables. The coins of which Dostoevsky's protagonist speaks of are not simply his own fortunes, or those of his country, but in the game of roulette itself, the metaphor for the gambles of livelihoods lost by a countryman's generals out of which the money they gamble is sanctified and made valuable through war. Twitter is caught in the same moral trap, at once needing to be gentlemanly about their race issues while their entire economy, morality, and internet entertainment industry continues to be sanctified, and paid for, by black on black crime. And in some ways, this is true of all those in the "free world", those living in Western capitalist economic zones, who believe in the false morality of Western Hip Hop acts. Dostoevsky writes of the violence:

"In a word, he must look upon the gaming-table, upon roulette, and upon trente et quarante, as mere relaxations which have been arranged solely for his amusement. Of the existence of the lures and gains upon which the bank is founded and maintained he must profess to have not an inkling. Best of all, he ought to imagine his fellow-gamblers and the rest of the mob which stands trembling over a coin to be equally rich and gentlemanly with himself, and playing solely for recreation and pleasure. This complete ignorance of the realities, this innocent view of mankind, is what, in my opinion, constitutes the truly aristocratic. [...]

On the other hand, I saw a Frenchman first win, and then lose, 30,000 francs cheerfully, and without a murmur. Yes; even if a gentleman should lose his whole substance, he must never give way to annoyance. Money must be so subservient to gentility as never to be worth a thought. Of course, the supremely aristocratic thing is to be entirely oblivious of the mire of rabble, with its setting; but sometimes a reverse course may be aristocratic to remark, to scan, and even to gape at, the mob (for preference, through a lorgnette), even as though one were taking the crowd and its squalor for a sort of raree show which had been organised specially for a gentleman's diversion."[28]

What gives the game its value, and what separates the aristocrat and general from the plebeian soldier, is his relationship to war. The general, for whom the sacrifices of his soldiers give light and value to his battles and his hordes of coins, must remain stoic in times of war, of risk, of gambles. The soldier, the plebian, must not. Forbidden by law to forego the stoicness of war strategy, it is through his passion that the spoils of war are sanctified as he imagines himself as stoic as his leaders, while they themselves slowly prove to be more emotional, and less gentlemanly, than their soldiers.

Cormac McCarthy poses the question of gentlemanliness in a different way. Rather than ask whether or not he is a gentleman, or an aristocrat, the judge in McCarthy's Blood Meridian asks of his soldiers of whether the coins are false and real coins, of what makes a war a real war, or a fake one, whether a man can become subsumed by the war, and whether it is a war to begin with.

"The coin, Davy, the coin, whispered the judge. He sat erect and raised his hand and smiled around. The coin returned back out of the night and crossed the fire with a faint high droning and the judge's raised hand was empty and then it held the coin. There was a light slap and it held the coin. Even so some claimed that he had thrown the coin away and palmed another like it and made the sound with his tongue for he was himself a cunning old malabarista and he said himself as he put the coin away what all men knew that there are coins and false coins. In the morning some did walk over the ground where the coin had gone but if any man found it he kept it to himself and with sunrise they were mounted and riding again. [...]

The good book says that he that lives by the sword shall perish by the sword, said the black.

The judge smiled, his face shining with grease. What right man would have it any other way? he said.

The good book does indeed count war an evil, said Irving.

Yet there's many a bloody tale of war inside it. It makes no difference what men think of war, said the judge. War endures. As well ask men what they think of stone. War was always here. Before man was, war waited for him. The ultimate trade awaiting its ultimate practitioner. That is the way it was and will be. That way and not some other way.[...]"[29]

War, to McCarthy and his God, the judge, simply do not exist without each other. It is in one another that man finds meaning, that man wages his life upon, for we would not do things in God's name were it not for war.

Brown reached into his pocket and came up with a handful of coins. He laid a two and a half dollar gold piece on the bench. Now, he said. I'm payin you two and a half dollars.

The farrier looked at the coin nervously. I dont need your money, he said. You cant pay me to butcher that there gun.[...]

In the floor of the scow was a small coin. Perhaps once lodged under the tongue of some passenger. He bent to fetch it. He stood up and wiped the grit from the piece and held it up and as he did so a long cane arrow passed through his upper abdomen and flew on and fell far out in the river and sank and backed to the surface again and began to turn and to drift downstream. He faced around, his robes sustained about him. He was holding his wound and with his other hand he ravaged among his clothes for the weapons that were not there and were not there. A second arrow passed him on the left and two more struck and lodged fast in his chest and in his groin. They were a full four feet in length and they lofted slightly with his movements like ceremonial wands and he seized his thigh where the dark arterial blood was spurting along the shaft and took a step toward the shore and fell sideways into the river. [...]

The fool was no longer there but another man and this other man he could never see in his entirety but he seemed an artisan and a worker in metal. The judge enshadowed him where he crouched at his trade but he was a coldforger who worked with hammer and die, perhaps under some indictment and an exile from men's fires, hammering out like his own conjectural destiny all through the night of his becoming some coinage for a dawn that would not be. It is this false moneyer with his gravers and burials who seeks favor with the judge and he is at contriving from cold slag brute in the crucible a face that will pass, an image that will render this residual species current in the markets where men barter. Of this is the judge judge and the night does not end."[30]

It is in this predicament that we find ourselves in as signs of the prophet Jonah become the norm. Much like the plastic that pollutes our waters that will in later generations be unearthed by older species as signs of our existence buried away in the earth's crust, so too have the true fruits of war been the consumer goods we consume. Lodged away as symbols of free trade in literature, the true question at the heart of the Russia-Ukraine war is not of the nature of war itself, or of man's ego, but of its necessity when the wars fought to open up international borders to the products of American and Western European free trade have subsumed national identities altogether, as <u>DISPOSABLE SOLDIER</u> by our anonymous friend displays. What is a spoil of war determined by, after all, if not the war it would inevitably be consumed for?

The diary begins with our soldier quickly writing off the supposed gains that communist Russia could have offered the Russian people as he describes his first day at the Russian recruitment office, and afterwards, the meaninglessness of the pre-war rituals of religion once announcing the faith and prosperity of a spiritually able nation.

"During the day, they issued us uniforms and handed out humanitarian aid bags from the Moscow mayor, containing all sorts of small items: a toiletry kit with disposable razors, a toothbrush, toothpaste, shaving cream, underwear, t-shirts, socks, and other such necessities. The bag itself was sturdy and spacious, much larger than the old Soviet-era kitbag.[...]

Midday, a nun from a monastery appeared at the recruitment office to see us off. She spoke to us as if we were heroes going to defend our Motherland from the enemy. The nun blessed anyone who wished and distributed amulets: icons, belts, and other monastery souvenirs that were supposed to protect us from injury and death. Many of us were believers, so even a year later, I would still see these amulet belts on soldiers from various units."

Despite him and his crew's avid patriotism for the motherland, war had not yet begun to broil, nor the patriotism it could instill or destroy, until alcohol was introduced into the lives of the Russian soldiers. In our consumerist societies, alcohol, which was often a necessary replenishment for the Russian soldiers, is one of the few things we can buy to bring us together. In an era where the spoils of war brought home by fathers to their sons, books and the meat that represents the strength of a nation, instead is carried to homes via pirated book sites and Amazon, consumer goods have strangely become simultaneously valued and valueless. Their value lies not in their material need or use, but rather in the value that has been prescribed to the item through the fame that it gives its owner on social media - its cultural value is fully virtual, and most often, associated with the value rappers and rap associated bodies have to the item. The wars our fathers and the West fought for have culminated in this individual success, that of their effort and struggle to be negated by the complete innecessity of war in free trade societies. The sight of young Americans not buying or drinking alcohol is not a sign or coin that represents their health, but that represents their solitude. In an era and generation where each person's reality and consumer identity is tailored to match their neurosis, alcohol is the only hope we have of breaking free from them. Once alcohol is denied to the Russian soldiers whose identity is more owed to the products living in Russia's free trade agreements granted them than to Russian culture or tradition itself does the war truly begin. So unprepared were the soldiers for the real warfare that during war games with one another they simply yelled "bang-bang" at each other. The only thing that continued to make them Russian was the ethnicity of the liquor store they shopped at.

"On another occasion, we had a "training battle." We went out to a field that the local governor had kindly provided, divided into two teams, dug shallow "trenches," and began "shooting" at each other with blank rounds, one at a time. During these exercises, some of us performed "genius" tactical moves, flanking the enemy. Our guys played as if they were a recon-sabotage group, sneaking into enemy lines and "taking down" a few soldiers. It was all easy, simple, and fun. There was no real danger to life.

How foolish we must have looked then. [...]

A general would arrive – the political officer of the academy or some other district – and his song would begin [...] Even then, it was clear what was going on in this comrade's head and what priorities he had established in this speech. – "And, most importantly, a soldier of the Russian Army must, in all his actions, be worthy of our great Motherland! A soldier must maintain discipline! Obey the orders of commanders and do nothing that would discredit the military honour of our army! And what do I see instead? Huh!? Every evening: a huge, green line! At the Krasnoe & Beloe liquor store!"

The men continued to bicker amongst each other as the thin veil of Russian aristocracy and democracy that once brought them together slowly flickers away as they lose the drugs that bind young men's lunacy and solitude.

"There was enough alcohol to last us a couple of days on the train, so many of us only sobered up at our destination. Throughout the journey, we could hear Nefrit playing his guitar and singing old favourites, which he, as usual, never finished; discussions about how awful the "Ukrops" (a derogatory term for Ukrainians) were and how we would defeat them all; conversations about life and God, and history.

"Do you believe in God?" Tush (Ink), a soldier who considered himself Orthodox, asked me.

"No," I replied.

"Good heavens, and I'm going to war with this man! How can you not believe in God? Are you even Russian?"

"And what about Ofis?" I asked, pointing to a stocky guy with an Asian face on the next bunk. "He's Muslim. Doesn't he bother you?"

"Well, even though he's Muslim, he believes in God! But you don't! [...]

But no one ever really figured out what happened. Whose order was it to hit Nefrit in the eye? Did he provoke it or not? We spent the whole evening drinking and arguing about "principles," but the whole situation remained utterly senseless."

God I love Russians. Even when writing simple journals, they make literary masterpieces. As the soldiers feel the pain and weight of riding in their military wagons known as Urals, the reality of the Ukrainian landscape sets in as our narrator sees himself confronted not simply with a country still living in the reigns of the soviet and communist spirit, but of a republic whose whole identity came from its cultural and rural way of life, not its urban lack of life and consumerist habits. This is until war finally breaks out.

"Making any extra movement in the Ural was a big problem. Standing up was a problem, changing seats was a problem, getting cigarettes out of your pocket was a problem. If your leg or backside went numb, that was a problem. If you needed to use the bathroom, that was a problem. The best solution you could come up with during a journey in an Ural was to try to sleep sitting up.

The scenery outside slowly changed. I like sitting near the side of a truck and observing what's happening outside. Russian and Ukrainian nature are similar, but the infrastructure was noticeably different. At first, we saw the well-maintained and civilized areas of the Russian provinces: paved roads and highways, small towns, shops, cafes, hotels, numerous road signs and indicators, bus stops, and other signs of urban life. This continued until we crossed the border and entered the territory of the "people's republics."

Here, in general, things looked similar, but it was evident that civilization was much weaker here. Buildings increasingly resembled Soviet architecture, bus stops were made of thick concrete, road signs became fewer and farther between, roads deteriorated, and consumer establishments like cafes and shops gradually disappeared.[...]

At that time, we didn't understand that war was about artillery. We didn't understand where our side was and where the enemy was. We didn't understand how far away the shots were coming from; we couldn't even distinguish outgoing fire from incoming fire by sound. We didn't understand anything at all. No one explained any of this to us. We understood only one thing: we couldn't do anything about it. [...]

Only later did we realize that it was Russian artillery firing near us. But we didn't see them. "Near" meant within a kilometre of us. What we considered incoming rounds were actually outgoing fire. But back then, we were sure of the opposite."

Much like war itself, its true nature is only revealed once we are subsumed to it. Faced with the horrors and passions of war, the Ukrainian struggle for independence suddenly is thrust upon this soldier as he realizes he has left the comfort of the free world along with the wars and trade routes designed to protect it. Trench warfare becomes the norm as Russian soldiers struggle to keep up with the brutality not of the mother nature we keep separate from us, but that instinct and drive of mother nature within us which all men recognize and describe as war.

"On the fifth day of our stay in Village U, I had the idea to build a latrine. I honestly dug a hole among the sunflowers, set up stumps of the right size for comfort. A piece of plywood with a hole made an excellent seat. Not like at home, of course, but not bad at all. The human body reacts to stressful situations in different ways. And for me, stress means constipation. Constipation can last up to a week. The body tries to absorb all the nutrients it can and not waste anything unnecessarily. That's why I really wanted to make a comfortable toilet, so I could finally feel human again. It was all for nought. I never got to use it.[...]

Our platoon was the first to move to the new location. We arrived in some forest, already in darkness. We spent a long time lugging our belongings from place to place before finally settling down for the night under the open sky. We didn't find any housing, and we only started exploring the surroundings in the morning. That morning, the temperature dropped just below freezing, and my sleeping bag was lightly covered with frost. When I crawled out of it, it softly crunched. Beautiful, simply beautiful! Ah, if only this were a vacation in nature – it would have been just perfect! But alas, it's only perfect when you can always return home, to civilization. [...]

And again, the loading of belongings, again the Ural, crammed full of duffel bags and people in body armor and helmets, with rifles. Again, we were going "nowhere." We took only the most necessary things with us, leaving one person to guard everything else in Village P – the most useless comrade from the army's point of view – Shesternya. He had enough firewood and food to survive alone. But even then, many laughed at him. He couldn't light a stove by himself, couldn't maintain the fire, couldn't cook food. I'm not exactly a survival expert either, but compared to him, I was Bear Grylls."

Bear Grylls is mentioned as the reality of modernity, or postmodernity, continues to rear its head - even when fighting against Americans and the West, Russian soldiers compare themselves to Western men who, through the internet, are universal symbols of masculinity. Civilization, or the idea of it, continues to be reinforced, and is a product of, access to manufactured, high quality consumerist goods. Most importantly, the internet, and access to its civility, means access to the female bodies women posted on it that men can get high off of. What does civility then mean, if not to, as the aristocrat did in Dotoevesky's <u>The Gambler</u>, react to our steady influx of war footage through social media with immobile levels of apathy, as if we never lost our humanity by seeing it transmitted as entertainment to be exploited for our own sense of morality in the process? Is the act of the American social media protest the aristocratic gesture, a sign of our absolute civility and nobility in the world of free trade, or are the negation of these protests signs of plebeian disregard, "conservative" sentiment, as a whole? Are we all trapped under the same moral constrictions the Russian soldiers, our supposed enemies, through free trade, are? Or is instead the protest a true sign of immorality, as our own egos take precedence over the casualties of war? What is war, and civility for that matter, if our nuns and mother Russia herself, are accessible through TikTok and TikTok alone, as the sight of war becomes meaningless when women adorn themselves with the spoils of war accessible to men only through social media?

"There was a small potbelly stove in the cellar, which we immediately put to use. We ruthlessly broke apart the beehive frames and spent the first week heating the stove with them. It was heartbreaking. Someone calculated that each frame was worth about a hundred rubles. The apiary's owner had spent years diligently crafting these frames, and now they were being used as firewood. We were heating the stove with money and the beekeeper's labour. And

there were a lot of frames and beehives: about a hundred hives, with a dozen frames for each hive. Nevertheless, it was still very cold at night.

Every night I cursed myself for not bringing a sleeping bag. [...]

The barrel stove turned out monstrous. After several days of unholy rituals of makeshift production and dances with a tambourine, hammer, and cow dung, this infernal contraption was born. A hellish spawn. Ugly, terrifying, leaky, smeared with shit – a Frankensteinian monster. But reliable and fully functional. We made it ourselves, and that was good. While we lived at the apiary, this stove reliably heated our garage; sometimes it even got too hot, like in a sauna."

Even the age-old spoils of war, meat, become inaccessible through the modern spoils of war and the technology that drives stakes between generations, of which the old refuse to accept their age and the young are left to, by the old, be held unfit for the responsibility the young are destined to bear.

"And once, we personally saw a wild boar. Not just a boar, but a huge boar! Fresh snow had just fallen, covering the hillside, and there it was – a massive boar running through the undergrowth, clearly visible. Well, we didn't bother it – we weren't about to go after it across a minefield anyway.[...]

We were busy with another distribution of supplies that Lineika had brought us. Instant noodles, grains, water, and other things. Tuz was dividing everything among the squads, and I took a box of zucchini caviar to carry it to the cellar. I had just taken my first step when a whistling sound passed over our heads. Half a second later – a booming explosion. We called this a "prilyot" (arrival/incoming)."

The sheer absurdity of the war becomes apparent as it did for Americans when the soldiers begin to argue over lost platitudes of the Russian identity, soldiers no longer subsuming themselves and gaining spiritual victories as a communist republic as the Chinese or Stalinists did. Rather than fight for the motherland, it is instead Putin in whom the soldier puts his trust in to stop the Western armies who themselves provided them with the access to the instant noodles and Bear Grylls references of the Western world. The question of why Europe is even involved in the war is even further out of the picture than that of Americans wanting to bring suffering to the Russian people. They too are suffering the costs of the lifestyle created by free trade by fighting a war against it all while Putin tries to revive conservative Russian nationalism in a generation raised without it.

"Between shelling, Kryuk and I would have all sorts of conversations at our post:

"- Russia is sending its people to their deaths to seize the territory of another country."

"- You see, this is our land. It has always been ours. These cities were built by our people, by the Russian tsars! We're just taking back what has always belonged to us. It was stolen from us – and we're taking it back."

"- People live on this land who have chosen their own path – a different path of development. They don't want to live the way Russia does."

"- There aren't people living on this land, there are Nazis. They kill people just for speaking Russian. Ukrainians want to be in Europe, yeah, right! Who'd let them in there! Ukrops are thieves and murderers, they always have been. Uncle Vova (Putin) won't let them get away with this."

"- Excuse me, but I think the thieves and murderers are the ones who sent us here. Putin is the main thief and murderer."

"- Tell me, what would you do if NATO bases were located near your house? The Americans want to destroy Russia, they want you to suffer. Taking this territory is the only way to ensure the safety of our children. Just you wait, Uncle Vova is going to launch nuclear missiles and wipe all these Ukrops off the face of the earth."[...]

We were incredibly bored. In the evenings, we would have a movie night on someone's phone, the whole squad together. There weren't many movies, but we had no choice. We would place the phone on a table near the stove, settle in comfortably with our tea, and watch together. The neighbouring squad watched a TV series. Sometimes, to entertain ourselves somehow, I would tell my comrades "fairy tales." First, "The Tale of Fedot the Archer, a Dashing Young Fellow." Then I moved on to retelling the plots of BioWare games. I recounted the stories of Dragon Age: Origins and Mass Effect.

I wasn't a very good storyteller, but the guys liked it – they turned out to be decent "fairy tales." There was nothing else to do anyway."

War eventually is re-introduced to the soldiers as a board game the disposable soldier played growing up. The game, made in Poland, ironically enough becomes the way by which the soldiers escape from the constant shelling of real war - and unlike in this one, the enemies in the board game conflict are easy to write off as subhuman - they are aliens from outer space.

"I also missed board games terribly. I had some experience playing Nemesis, and I had repeatedly explained the rules of the game to my friends, so I decided out of boredom to recreate this game here. Plywood became the game board, and cardboard from boxes became the locations, tokens, and markers. A book of Ukrainian fairy tales from the latrine was torn apart and turned into ability cards, item cards, and event cards. I recreated the game characters and their abilities, items, and objectives from memory. Instead of miniatures for characters and monsters, we used shell casings and cartridges. It wasn't the original Nemesis, but a perfectly playable creation, made on the fly in a shed from a combination of wood and, well, you know. Two guys agreed to play with me – and we even won the game (thankfully, I made it a bit easier than the original). All the players enjoyed it, but we only played it once – after all, board games of this kind aren't for everyone. My creation quickly faded into oblivion, but I have very fond memories of it."

The only things remaining of mother Russia and her past were drunkards and the women who in the eyes of the men continued in their ignorance. War, and civilization, can then be said, are simply summarized by the way by which one accesses, and justifies, pornography.

"That's how we spent almost the entire second half of winter. Defender of the Fatherland Day was approaching (god, how I hate this holiday now), followed by the anniversary of the start of the "Special Military Operation." The approach of these holidays made us very anxious. About a week before them, Lineika arrived and announced

that there would soon be an assault near the City of M.

"Well, soldiers! Congratulations to all of you on Defender of the Fatherland Day, valiant soldiers of the Russian army! Today I permit you to have a few drinks. Relax, but don't overdo it. Tomorrow morning, we might be going on the assault."

"How? When? Will they come for us? What are our orders?"

"So, here's the plan. We take only weapons, armour, ammunition, shovels, and a couple of days' worth of food. Don't load up or leave without my personal presence, I'll give you the order myself."

With that, he finished and left. We hoped that this would be the end of the story. Surely, everyone will be celebrating Defender of the Fatherland Day now, and there won't be any assault! It would be madness to send everyone into an assault drunk! And Lineika's words were imprinted in our memory: "Don't load up or leave without my personal presence." So, our evening continued as usual, with vodka and music.[...]

The instinct for self-preservation pushed our senior guys to argue. No one wanted to die, so all ten of us yelled obscenities at the poor driver, who was made the scapegoat in this situation. The driver had no authority over us; he was simply relaying the command's orders. While this argument was going on, no one noticed how the quietest one among us, nicknamed "Shelk" (Silk), quietly packed his duffel bag, put in a couple of days' worth of food and water, took his weapons and ammunition, put on his body armour and white camouflage suit, and, without saying a word to anyone, got into the truck to go to the assault.

Shelk was the most humble, quiet, and reserved among us. But behind this modesty hid a great rage: Shelk's brother had been killed in the war with the Ukrainians, and now he thirsted for revenge. He once told me: "I want to strangle a Ukrop with my own hands."

A few people knew about Shelk's desire, but we thought that common sense and the instinct for self-preservation would be stronger than his thirst for revenge. We were wrong. That evening, Shelk was the only one completely sober. He knew what he had to do. He chose his own fate."

When I was in high school, I often daydreamed of going to war, because I wondered if I needed to participate in such a conflict to have my depression, my isolation I felt to the world, validated by such violence. It was this violence, of a personal history that Americans seemed to not have, that drew me away from them. In my final year of college, when the war in Ukraine broke out, I began to take up my rosary again, praying in public as I hoped to find a way to mourn for those lost in the conflict. I have, since then, wondered which side I am supposed to mourn for, if, as an American, I should have sympathy for the people of Ukraine over Russia. In his diary, the disposable soldier speaks of "the 500ths", a group of men who retreated during their first shelling experience but went along with Shelk to the assault. They gave them that nickname as a joke so the men who stayed in the shelling could feel braver than they were, adopting the irony of postmodernism as their own as they realized the meaninglessness of the term in age without war, but subsumed by its mindless violence. Shelk and the men who accompanied him in a sense of brotherly camaraderie died as even their leader, Lineika, refused to call home to a fallen soldier's wife, as if the generals who sent them to war would care about her, and men continue to identify not with old military generals, but with themselves and their comrades.

"'The commanders are fucking bastards. They just sent us to be slaughtered. It's a fucking nightmare.'

We never again laughed at our "five-hundredths." After all, the "five-hundredths" had participated in that meat grinder. And we hadn't. Now we were the "five-hundredths."

Kulich the puppy whimpered incessantly, missing his owner.

That evening, we mourned Suleiman. We drank a shot of vodka and left another shot on the table, covered with a piece of black bread. The mournful mood lingered for several more days. We didn't feel like doing anything. Someone had to inform his wife that her husband had died. Some of us asked Lineika to call her, but he refused.

"The headquarters will handle it, they'll call." [...]

After a while, we learned that the neighbouring company

71

had recorded a video message and posted it online. In their video message, they talked about the meat grinder and demanded that the commanders be held accountable. This video message quickly spread throughout the entire battalion, reaching us and the ZGT (information security) officers. An investigation began.

We called our relatives and friends. We asked them to spread this video message, to create public awareness. What we were hoping to achieve with this, I didn't understand myself."

Soldiers slowly begin to remember their own importance as their generals come to fail them. In the last moments of 4chan and this soldier's first tour, cofi anon's translation reveals that our disposable soldier returns to Russia himself unscathed with the battalion puppy remaining as the only spoil of war from the battle. He ends his tour reminiscing, with nostalgia, on the innocence of that age, quoting a famous song, that much like Jack Black's meme power, ushered in the end of a saga. For if Einstein stated that WWIV would be fought with sticks and stones, the soundtrack to WWIII would inevitably be that of a descendant of a spoil of war, an African slave, teaching Mark Zuckerberg, he who decides war, how to serenade his wife by telling her about how he wishes to ejaculate on her face. There were no poets left to capture the serenity of peace, for the spoils of war became peace herself, and the soundtrack to the Shrek movies she supposedly inspired. 10 years ago, Mark Zuckerberg, today "the white man", would have been T-Pain's ally, and since then, the greatest casualties of our lives have been the lives and lifestyles lost during the creation of the COVID pandemic.

"Some slept, some smoked, passing the ashtray from hand to hand. I sat by the tailgate, watching the road. When day broke, the column stopped near a supermarket. Everyone began to wake up and stir. We could get out, use the bathroom, go to the store, have lunch —and, of course, everyone ran for alcoholic beverages. Finally, real alcohol from a store! Green figures in a long line carried rustling bags back to the vehicles, clinking with every step.

When the column continued on its way, a drinking session began in the Ural. This wasn't a wake anymore—this was a celebration! We turned on the music. Cognac and whiskey were passed around. I quickly mixed up energy drinks and juice into a cocktail. Our spirits were high, and each of us looked to the future with the hope that everything would be alright!

Somebody once told me the world is gonna roll me
I ain't the sharpest tool in the shed
She was looking kind of dumb with her finger and her thumb
In the shape of an "L" on her forehead

Well, the years start coming and they don't stop coming
Fed to the rules and I hit the ground running
Didn't make sense not to live for fun
Your brain gets smart but your head gets dumb

So much to do, so much to see
So what's wrong with taking the back streets?
You'll never know if you don't go (GO!)
You'll never shine if you don't glow

Hey, now, you're an all-star, get your game on, go play
Hey, now, you're a rock star, get the show on, get paid
And all that glitters is gold

Only shooting stars break the mould"[31]

HUNTER BIDEN'S DRUG ADDICTION AND THE END OF THE DEMOCRATIC PARTY

"I have always been struck, in America, by an emotional poverty so bottomless, and a terror of human life, of human touch, so deep that virtually no American appears able to achieve any viable, organic connection between his public stance and his private life. This failure of the private life has always had the most devastating effect on American public conduct, and on black-white relations. If Americans were not so terrified of their private selves, they would never have become so dependent on what they call "The Negro Problem".

[NO WAY OUT, J. MANKIEWICZ – 1950]

They said it wasn't nice to say "n*gger". N*gger! N*gger! N*gger! Poor little n*gger kids, love the little n*gger kids. Who loved me? Who loved me?

This problem, which they invented in order to safeguard their purity, has made of them criminals and monsters, and it is destroying them. And this, not from anything Blacks may or may not be doing, but because of the role of a guilty and constricted white imagination has assigned to the Blacks."[32]

-James Baldwin, *I Am Not Your Negro*

There is little that has been said about Hunter Biden, and his infamous laptop, that has not been said, speculated on, or written of - the case is by now so infamous, so synonymous with America, that is to say, with the domestic policies of America, not its worldwide image, that it is difficult not to draw light on a subject that, much like a horse reeking of still death, whose corpse and carcass lingers with maggots and flies flying over it to signal rotting flesh, stinking life, and a spectacle all the more watchable for those who discover said corpse, cannot merely be understood through prose alone. Much like a detective discovering a crime scene, so too are all the intricacies, the ironies, and racial politics all wrapped up in the life and fate of one man's, and his father's, failures, agonies, and successes, a perfect metaphor for the collective failure of Francis Fukuyama's so-called end of history and perfection of the American democracy: much like the journals of the Russian soldier posted on 4chan, so too is our collective history, relationship to the internet, and the West, trapped completely in the metaphor that is the leaked images of the president of America's son, consumed by drug addiction, and worse than that, crack, that, much like the failure of Putin to create a war in age born without Russian nationalism, captures the complete failure of the American public, and the Democratic party, to truly usher in the end of history, and furthermore, catapult the country into the 21st century. It was not just that the laptop revealed what is true about ourselves, or the assumptions we hold to be true about democracy, but rather, than in pardoning Hunter Biden, the Democratic party itself, failing to hold itself accountable not for its own country, but simply its own children, that the party itself attested to one singular thing alone: its inability to, in holding themselves accountable, hold Donald Trump accountable in the same light: for the only difference between Trump and Hunter, apart from their character and morality is Hunter's, and the Democratic party's, necessity, to keep private the facts about American life Trump celebrates, publicly, as the world over has known America to be. I, for one, know all too well the rumors in Venezuela held about YouTuber Mr. Beast: not that he is a pedophile, as is believed by the American public of its celebrities and politicians, but rather, that the UN secretly wishes to kill Mr. Beast because Mr. Beast did in one YouTube video what the UN, and Hunter Biden, have been claiming to do for years: build 100 water wells in the lands of the third world. It is in this case that it was not simply Biden that failed his son, nor all the Americans who having parents like Biden, found themselves much like him, strung out on the streets of their country despite its and their own successes, but rather, that in pushing the country into the 21st century, the American family failed at bringing their children, offspring, and eventual harbingers of life, liberty, and the pursuit of happiness, those same values that the founding fathers held so dear to their hearts. Perhaps it is for this sole reason alone that the whole spectacle was met with such ironic laughter from my generation: the transgression to be had here comes solely from the fact that in public, crack has always been relegated to black America; the fact that a white boy, the president's son, was caught using it, must therefore mean we have been lying to ourselves about the nature of the drug all along.

I myself was part of the zeitgeist that held Hunter to such an esteem, part of the overflowing well of democracy that united violently against the so-called Venezuelan migrant threat, not particularly for any other reason other than that Americans force you to do so; I was only able to humanize the man, now known for his indie sleaze lifestyle only imaginable to those who have walked through the hallowed halls of American democracy, part of the generation known by all for their inability to watch cable news but that falls for Hip Hop based Twitter propaganda anyways. It was under these conditions that Hunter was able to finally open himself up to the world, coming to meet with Andrew Callaghan and do a three hour, Oprah style interview, filled with such sincerity and molestation of the so-called free press that such intimacy could not be regarded as anything else but mere miracle; what Hunter Biden saw in the man in whom he would trust his public life to still remains a mystery to me. What does not linger in my mind, however, is that the marginal characters me and my generation laugh at through Channel 5's videos, their marginal ways and unchecked "mental health" episodes simply a reflection of a country with a profound neurosis leaves me with is that these characters are not jokes, marginal, or stereotypes in Biden's imagination: they were a part of his lived reality, a direct threat, assault, assisination, and re-enforcement of his character that he hid, and lived with, each waking moment of his life. It would be then remiss of me not to mention the utmost irony of the president's son, accused of working with so-called "propaganda" machines such as the New York Times, whose father, the president of the United States of America, who even though failed at addressing the living conditions of the American ghettos still managed to pass more progressive legislation at 82 than any other president in the country in recent history, who was labeled as bygone and out of date by these same so-called "media outlets", would be protected by the man known as Andrew Callaghan. It was this same man who would reverse the game on these legacy media apparatuses, leaving them as bygone and unnecessary in American life, independently, as all Americans should strive to do, when he gained the upper hand on them by interviewing the president's son only for the New York Times to label him as a meek "RV YouTuber". Despite being the man of the son who history passed by, the entire media apparatus of this country, which revels in celebrating the legacy of acclaimed rapper, crack dealer, and most likely fed-backed informant, Pusha T, had no sympathy for either white man in this YouTube interview: that would mean both journalistic and literary credentials from the New York Times, a now out of date publishing house that has more in common with common tabloids from ten years ago than a serious literary publication.

"Consider the appalling condition of the United States at this time. If you can make your way through the New York Times, which I find very difficult because it is now scarcely grammatical and the syntax has largely vanished but still is the best we got of its kind - the appalling things that you read about, the national proclivity for nonsense, not just in the sphere of political hatred, but in very nearly everything else. And it comes because people cannot think. And in order to think you must remember the best that has been written,

the best that has been thought, the best that has been said. Without that it will all be hopeless. And since, for the most part, alas we don't have education like that anymore, particularly in the elite in the universities, particularly in the graduate schools, upon which I turned my back in '68, '69, and I never regretted it, but it may not matter in the end. But it may not matter in the end. All teaching can do is help. There has to be an initial gift or vocation. There has to be an initial impulse towards deep reading and it remains all but universal. It is too bad it cannot be fostered more than it is. It is too bad we allow it to be blocked out by all of the visual overbombardment of the age of the screen whether it be the computer screen or the television screen or the motion picture or what you will, virtual reality indeed, but it will survive. It will survive. [...] I can recall that [the parents of my Yale students] had read more before they reached Yale because it was easier to read in those days. [...] [Students] just need to be left alone and told there is nothing better for you to do than solitary reading."[33]

-Harold Bloom, 2002

Perhaps it is for this reason that, if we are to take Ralph Waldo Emerson's suggestion, that history is merely subjective, and that in the absence of reading or a history, that all can be said about history in the present is that is mere *belief* - that is to say, that until history is written as history and regarded as such, when the stories and tales we tell ourselves about who we are through our public figures is "set in stone", that we merely have religion - the history of the present - and in a feverishly religious society as our own, where the individualistic nature of American society takes precedence over any other, that the Hunter Biden laptop scandal did not take place in our collective history but simply became a matter of biography, of religion, a final and ultimate metaphor for the collective inability for the American public at large to deal, publicly, with the reality that the Cold War did not end, that it has continued into the 21st century, and most of all, that our elected leaders, nor is our public, in any way shape or form ready to collectively face such a momentous disaster as, despite the civil rights victories of the Biden administration have proved, the country simply has no moral backbone, or structure, by which to declare war let alone foster the strength necessary to wage a war of economic attrition against mother Russia; it is no longer the 20th century, Hunter Biden's drug use cannot be covered up like FDR's polio and the most lucrative story in the New York Post's history was uncovered by Americans who, in their simplicity, simply believed they were doing the right thing. Why we are still so divided has completely to do with the assertions that James Baldwin made years before; why, for example, Marjorie Taylor Greene's affairs[34] with gym trainers that cosplay as Russian street fighter character Zangief are never a point of contention, or why, for example, despite having different backgrounds Hunter Biden and J.D. Vance's communities have not yet been able to sympathize with their shared struggle of drug addiction still goes back to the so-called "Negro Problem", one fully viewed in the interview with Callaghan where Hunter Biden, still owing his identity to Delaware, must nevertheless contend with his state's place in having taken place in the Civil War in the first place. Can we really consider any of these leaders the harbingers of freedom? The upholders of democracy, not because of their own actions, domestically, because of ICE raids or trans rights, but because they simply have not found ways to blend their public lives with their personal ones? Can we consider the truth, in this day and age of American life, any more appealing to us than its lie?

Marjorie's men: The 46-year-old mother of three had an affair with polyamorous tantric sex guru Craig Ivey (left) before moving on to gym manager Justin Tway (right) while working at a gym in Alpharetta in 2012

It is strangely, in this way, that the communist didactic of the oppressor and the oppressed must be replaced by that of el-Hajj Malik el-Shabazz's field negro and house negro, for only his can hope to convey the public-private didactic of not only western but general life. There is little that could not be said about either political party's, Democrats and Republicans alike, ability to be house negroes; Trump himself is the final manifestation of such abhorrent monstrosities, a full display of the perversion of America that makes all those who look up to him identify with him more than with themselves, a possibility only possible by the Democratic party's own inability to do the same. It is with them that the class tensions that plague America, those of the liberal college educated elite, privileged enough to be crack addicts but skilled enough to be the heads of boards in multinational charities, arises. It was not just the medical system that killed off most of the American middle class, that failed its citizens, but that also failed the child of the President of the world's largest military empire. It was not just the American family that failed at fostering change, from Biden failing to read his own son's essay from Yale about the effect of crack legislation that failed, but the fact that the healthcare system could even fail the president's son, with the president himself, despite all the advancements and progress he tried to bring, failing at reforming the medical system and culture that gave his son such a tragic, lonely, and desperate life that the American public themselves could not confront, instead making religious spectacle out of our failing cities and healthcare system instead. If even the president's son could not bring hope or change to a nation, if even father could not take care of son, if both needed to safeguard their purity, and the purity of the country, in the process, who would?

"*Shlyapa spent a long time in treatment, but in the end, his vision returned. Having gone through all of this, he admitted that he now agreed with my liberal views: a genocide of the Russian people is taking place, and Russia is the one orchestrating it. Russia wants its citizens dead.*"[35]

Hunter Biden himself looked, in the interview, still constrained by the white imagination, to prop up his own drug use, and his family's response to it, on his family's history and place, culturally within the United States, as Irish Catholics, still believing in the purity of the country, not seeing himself as the full manifestation of the entirety of the sin contained within it. A family man, Hunter, whose name rings with the love a father has for his child trapped in the immaturity a father always sees his son through the lens of, traveled the world hoping, in vain, through the United Nations and the like, to save people from the empires the West wrought on them, only for him to come home, become a symbol of worldwide money laundering, but most of all, to escape from the despair, and look to justify him and his father's actions, much like the leeches who joined him during his drug addiction, through crack cocaine, alcoholism, but most of all, prostitutes, those women of the night who know only the utmost truth about the men in power of our society, of whom Hunter Biden never spoke of perhaps because they were the ones who knew not only the most about him, but about the country we live in, in the first place. What were the circumstances that led to such an American story? Was it the crack or the black community's response to the drug? Was it black America or the crime bills created in "protecting" them, and the country's, supposed puritan image? Who failed Joe Biden first? His son, or his own guidance? His country, or his family? Can we even say which, or, is it in trying to find an answer, that we simply seek to justify the crime, tragedy, or honesty, altogether?

Hunter Biden's laptop contained within it all of these questions, all the assumptions and insecurities we had of ourselves, and of Joe Biden's presidency alone, the anxiety around our failed leaders and their inability to have any meaningful cybersecurity, the public's own ability to usurp the position of our elected leaders as those of the most powerful nation on the planet earth, the role of social media and news coverage, our so-called negro or migrant problem, but most of all, who the Democratic party is, who the Deep State or media is supposed to protect, and what exactly their role is in American democracy. It was both Republican and Democratic alike that saw their suffering and despair toiled away inside the images of Hunter, the artists of New York City gatekept from its art world coinciding with the sleaze of Republican voters to unite against it, never in fact keeping intact any semblance or shred of morality, or political position, to begin with, the mere spectacle, laughter, and joy of the laptop simply relegated to political theatre as each side, looking to reaffirm their inability for their despair to be captured by either the legacy media or partisan politics looked to, in removing Hunter Biden's humanity from the story, be assured they were more powerful, more moral, and if anything, more deserving to be in the control of the country than both him, his father, and the Democratic party as a whole, for the laptop was nothing new, but rather, confirmed the assumptions about corruption within the party the country believed the media was helping cover up. Trump, for example, can be a ne'er do well and criminal mastermind because of his sincerity; Hunter Biden, however, is labeled a criminal and painted in the same light, negatively, for the same reasons, not for anything other than the fact that we are supposed to trust the Democratic party's moral assertions while Donald Trump never gave the country a reason to trust him to be anything but himself in the first place. Perhaps this is the Democratic party's ultimate failing, a party that, despite having billions, and possibly trillions, to its name, is currently being overthrown by the Irish American Steve Bannon, a man whose mere demeanor is exemplative of his disinterest in being pure, but most of all, whose lies can be believed because it is simply part of the American immaturity we have all come to know and love.

"That's why it's called WWIII, cause there's a whole mothafuckin' war going on right now and they ain't telling us shit. We don't even know whose side is what. Whole war going on. Fortunately for us it's simple. It's not even complicated. White people don't get nervous. It ain't about race this time. Mhhm mhhm. Ain't about money this time. No no. This time it's the lie vs. the truth. Just that simple. [...] I'm not here to say what side is the best sides I'm just saying them the sides. [...] Y'all always gotta have a proper respect for your opps. One of these sides don't respect the opps. The lovers of truth - they don't give a fuuuuccckk about the lie. And they will tell you. 'This is the truth right here I don't give a fuck!' You'll tell them about the lie the lie ain't shit. Shit. Lies run the world. Gotta respect it. Lies run the world. For every time one lie get told one million people make one million dollars. For every lie. You know who the fuck pay for it? Whoever the fuck don't know its a lie. That's who the fuck pay for it. [...] Cause the liar he'll get you to believe some shit. They don't stop there. [...] They said there's a chicken wing shortage but we got plenty of thighs."[36]

-Katt Williams

So despite not being a race war, it is the mere presence of America's necessity on race to construct a morality by which this war will be won or lost, whether it be the one in Ukraine or the domestic one, for if there is one thing I am assured of it is the knowledge that Hunter Biden is ready to go to war for his children's future. What exactly we will do about the kids is still a mystery, who we will tell them we are or were a matter of complete subjectivity; the only question remains is that of what it means to be a successful American because it was not Andrew that brought Hunter to him, but rather, the questions Anrew asked about what it meant to be an American, and furthermore, a *man*, in his film *Dear Kelly* that made Hunter Biden know he was not alone in searching for the meaning of the truth about American life.[37]

FAKE NEWS

This still, however, leaves the question that everyone seems to forget but completely willing to ask: how exactly did Donald Trump gain his rise to power? I myself still posit than the answer lies within Harold's Bloom's <u>The American Religion</u> and Cormac McCarthy's <u>Blood Meridian</u> and their frankly accurate assessment of American socio-religious life but nevertheless the question still remains: not only why did the Democratic party fail at beating Trump, that is to say, why have modern women failed at leading men, but in addition, why are modern men failing at leading women?

It seems to me that this question traces its origins to the assisination of Dr. Martin Luther King for two particular reasons: TV, and TV advertisements, and, following his death, the way by which Americans campaigned through the so-called "black problem" without ever directly addressing it. Before King's death, and Reagan's rise to power, presidential campaign slogans were simple and direct; "I Like Ike", Kennedy's "Leadership for the 60s" or FDR's "The Man with the Heart, The Party for the Soul". They were direct and lacked the nostalgia by which Ronald Reagan, and his Californian Hollywood charisma, would come to dictate the next 50 or so years of American presidential candidacy. Nixon, who had run against the lawlessness of the 1960s in 1968 simply chose to adopt the post assisination depression of 1970s America as his own in '72, as did Carter and Ford, Regan came up with an ingenious solution: make an ad campaign strong, sincere, heartfelt, and nostalgic enough to make up for the fact that the country simply did not know what to do with itself after King's murder. He did this twice: first, in his first bid for election, having run as having "fixed" California and its hippie problem, alongside the Panthers in Oakland, and then again, in his second term, when he stated "It's morning again in America." Having slashled interest rates to make up for the despair in his ghettos and the failed promises of the Vietnam war, Reagean promised the American people that they would never have to look back into their past to be reminded of the despair of their present situation. Instead, through his reworking of American nostalgia, an everpresent sincerity matched with a state of perpetual grief often known as "despair", Reagan brought America back into its "golden age" and, eventually, the end of the cold war and the so-called communist threat.

The next 30 or 40 years would follow with political campaigns each one with the exact same messaging, a nostalgia rooted in necessitating a return to a pre-war America not to be reminded of anything but a private innocence that would be matched by campaign promises of something similar in the public eye; each one, whether it was Bill Clinton's promises to fix the wealth gap, be tougher on crime, or otherwise, were simply metaphors and ways to state "we would not like to be black in America" as part of a profound American desire for self-assurance was followed by economic policies of the same caliber: those damn Republicans are too selfish, and conservative, said the Democrat, we need higher taxes and government overreach. The Republicans said the same, but in the reverse: it would be the Democratic party who was too stupid to wave taxes on the rich that overpromised the American people, regardless of the fact both parties successively and efficiently both increased governmental and executive control and spending, precisely because of the desire for Americans to be reassured of their own morality by their elected leaders; innocence, and sincerity, was what was most desperately desired, and sold, alongside nostalgia, to the American people. At no point, however, did the country ever really change; the duality, however, of the questions of why Obama came to power, and, moreover, Trump's rise to power afterwards, have within them the, how shall we say, contemporary atrocities of American life, but most of all, the shame brought forth by the Democratic party, one which in private bullies union leaders like Sean O'Brien while in public claiming the affinity and illusionment of proto-facist women of the first world; nowhere is this more prevalent than in the most recent Oxford debate between men and women that had as its American guest Charlie Kirk and as its debate question "Has Donald Trump Gone Too Far?" Besides the fact Charlie Kirk is a borderline illiterate imbecile whose only fear is not the reverence of God but how his children will judge him and the country he raises him in, the one thing both men and women of either of this political aisle shared was not simply immaturity but the complete inability to comprehend either the role the Russia-Ukraine war has had on domestic American politics alongside the inability for either party to address made by plaintiff Katie Johnson against Trump; the simple rebuttals that the women could have made, that Charlie Kirk is a coward who will not debate an Econ student like Dean Withers famous for his viral TikTok debates because "econ majors are not exemplary of contemporary American college students", that he is simply, in many cases, too illiterate to read or follow even the most basic principles and tenets of the gospels, or, moreover, the very basic and simply statement "Donald Trump went too far when young girls on Epstein's island told him no and he kept going", were nowhere to be found: instead, the only thing both sides of the political isle could agree upon, even those who, I mean I have a hard time event taking myself seriously at this point. For a man who claims to value Western culture or society you'd think Charlie Kirk would quote a single Western intellectual at some point in his public speaking career, or that someone would have gone up to him and refuted his question of "What is a woman?" with "Do you think the young girls Donald Trump raped were old enough to be considered women when he raped them?"

Regardless, at the crux of a debate about the fate of the future of the Western world, the second female speaker opened up with an allegory as to how Donald Trump was like Donald Duck while the black queen of Oxford something or other was dressed up alongside her female counterparts in Disney princess dresses more tacky than ones seen at Quinceanera's in even the tackiest parts of Texas. The black woman was most likely, as in my experience, the most racist person in the room, whose mere presence shone light on the entirety of the hypocrisy of the debate, the fact being that while standing "against" white supremacy every single woman there only has value as an "educated" woman because she paid a white male institution, Oxford, to grant her value, only for "white" men like Charlie Kirk to tell her her education has no value because it makes him seen as the root of immorality in Western society as black men in America are seen as being; whatever the case may be, both sides could only agree on one thing: the opposite gender, each one represented by either the Democrats or Trump, were in no way fit to lead one another: the men unfit to lead the women and the women unfit to lead the men: neither, in any case, could justify the Ukraine war, not for geopolitical or domestic reasons, but because neither side was fit to lead. Charlie Kirk's sheer inability to read, alongside the women's complete and total immaturity, set the tone for what was once considered the bastion of modernity in the Western world.

This debate, strangely enough, originally set in motion by Hillary Clinton's presidential bid in 2008, was postponed by Obama's rise to power. While a lot has been said about the president, mostly due to his race and the fact American, especially Jewish, liberals, have a strange, almost sexual fetishization of him, as if to say, "finally, a black man I could see my daughter dating!" I am not sure as to if anyone has ever analyzed his presidency in earnest, nor, for that matter, taken an aracial lens to it or the presidents that came before him. For starters, it would be hard to imagine any presidential candidate running as a Democrat losing to the Republicans that election cycle: even the most staunch proponents of the cleansing of Islam from the Middle East could see the wars were made up failures of foreign policy by either Dick Cheney or George Bush, meaning Obama was essentially given a layup when he stated he would take the troops out of Iraq. This was still a distinctly "middle class", TV based America, one where the Democratic party's aesthetic was still defined by a Rust Belt aesthetic, not one based on wokeism and purity; to call the Iraq war anything less than ethnic cleansing would have been offensive, but to claim of American exceptionalism, and its endless innocence, was the only thing of which John McCain could rely on. This, of course, would fail, just as Putin, smart enough to recognize that he could use Biden's old age and lack of leadership to destabilize the United States by invading Ukraine during the Biden presidency, was spoken of during the 2008 debate between Obama and McCain, because Obama was not the first black American to run for president but he sure as hell was the most impressive. That is to say, in other words, that Trump's rise to power not in 2016 but in 2024 was already a point of contention in the 2008 presidential election, one which left the United States completely unable to combat the new Russian regime due to, as Putin found out during the Ukraine war, outdated worldviews completely inapplicable to the lives led by a generation raised on the internet.

These lives, quickly defined by Obama's presidency, were the lives me and my generation were raised under. I, for example, can clearly remember the tears rolling down the cheeks of the gay white liberal Jew the morning of Trump's election. Not only was I unfazed by this, having been of Venezuelan and/or Latino descent in an American suburb of Boston, I was, for the most part, shocked as to why anyone thought Trump couldn't win - from my point of view, the man was simply parroting the things every single comment section on the internet had been saying about me (Mexicans, which is what the Americans I went to elementary school all saw me as, whether openly or in private) and, in some other ways too, black Americans and Muslims, most of whom were seen as backwards by the white liberals I grew up around. I was not, unlike my classmates, shocked at his victory, but rather, shocked at their response to it; the inability for them to process it must mean, and have meant, that no matter what they claimed their beliefs were, we lived in entirely separate realities; I was considered "brown" in America, but perhaps, more accurately, it was not who I was, or who Obama meant to them, but rather, the idea about us that they had created for themselves that made it impossible for them to comprehend how Donald Trump, or for that matter, Obama, could have won in the first place. This, of course, leads us back to the question of how Obama became victorious over Clinton and the rest of the DNC in 2008, which to me seems as simple as the fact that, being young, and, being black, that is to say, not being of the elk of politician as apprehensive to helping dark skinned people in Chicago, he was simply the least corrupt member of the DNC to run for office, because we always remember the victories, but we seldom remember the races; the first question posed at the 2008 primary in Charleston, SC, sent in by video and broadcasted live on CNN, was, much like MLK's spectre, still lingering in the air 51 years later.

"So my question is we have a bunch of leaders who can't seem to do their job and when we pick people based on the issues that they represent but then they get in power and they don't do anything about it anyways. You're gonna spend this whole night talking about your views on issues, but the issues don't matter if when you get in power nothing's gonna get done. We have Congress and the president with like a 30% approval rating so clearly we don't think they're doing a good job. What's gonna make you any more affectual? Beyond all the platitudes and the stuff we're used to hearing, I mean, be honest with us. How are you going to be any different?"

-Zach Kempf to the DNC, 2008

"If the executive and legislative branches of the government were as concerned about the protection of our citizenship rights as the federal courts have been, then the transition from a segregated to an integrated society would be infinitely smoother. But we so often look to Washington in vain for this concern. [...] This dearth of positive leadership from the federal government is not confined to one particular political party. [...] The Democrats have betrayed it by capitulating to the prejudices and undemocratic practices of the southern Dixiecrats. The Republicans have betrayed it by capitulating to the blatant hypocrisy of right wing, reactionary northerners. [...] The hour is late. The clock of destiny is ticking out. We must act now,

before it is too late. [...]

I cannot close without stressing the urgent need for strong, courageous and intelligent leadership from the Negro community. We need a leadership that is 1957 calm and yet positive. This is no day for the rabble-rouser, whether he be Negro or white. (All right) We must realize that we are grappling with the most weighty social problem of this nation, and in grappling with such a complex problem there is no place for misguided emotionalism. (All right, That's right) We must work passionately and unrelentingly for the goal of freedom, but we must be sure that our hands are clean in the struggle. We must never struggle with falsehood, hate, or malice. We must never become bitter. I know how we feel sometime. There is the danger that those of us who have been forced so long to stand amid the tragic midnight of oppression—those of us who have been trampled over, those of us who have been kicked about—there is the danger that we will become bitter. But if we will become bitter and indulge in hate campaigns, the old, the new order which is emerging will be nothing but a duplication of the old order. (Yeah, That's all right)"

-Dr. Martin Luther King Jr., 1957, "Give Us the Ballot"

51 years since King expressed this dream, it had still yet to leak into the minds of American politicians, let alone academics, who, as far as I am concerned, especially in the era of DEI, for the most part, cannot name 3 Martin Luther King Jr. or el-Hajj Malik el-Shabbaz speeches but could name a myriad of anti-racism initiatives targeted at black women to make up for the fact that black men are, in America, not allowed to stand up for them; nevertheless, the DNC primary would slowly careen to the cliff of Obama vs. Hillary Clinton, a polite but amicable gesture won mostly by Obama's charisma, and, frankly, talent, something the Democratic party is still reconciling with. Thinking she could run on being a woman alone in 2016, I am still convinced Biden was forced to run in 2020 as the manifestation of the phrase "I have black friends" for the leader of the free world - only a party so tactless as them could lose, both times, to Donald J. Trump.

Having won spectacularly again against Mitt Romey, who himself did not how to identify himself to the American public, stuck at odds with being a Northern Liberal's version of a Republican while trying to provide Reaganesque nostalgia to southern Dixiecrats, Obama did not beat him because he was black, but because Obama was young and did a good job, something that, despite Clinton's success in the backgrounds of politics, meant she was sadly doomed to fail against Trump, not simply because of her lack of charisma or popular public policy, but because Donald Trump was simply who Hillary Clinton chose to be in private, publicly. His assured victory over her had very little to do with who either character is or was, or even who Obama was or is; having lost their ability to rely on the so-called "black question", the identity of the Republican party would simply be replaced by the election of irresponsibility, publicly, for the future of the nation, not through Hillary Clinton, but through Donald Trump. Lacking a rose tinted, nighttime sincerity of a children's storybook Reagan gave the Republican party, Trump's rise to power coincided with the failures of the Democratic party's, through Bill Clinton's trade deals, ability to either close the border, create meaningful social change, whether racially or otherwise, and, moreover, secure American job loss to overseas companies.

Obama, it seems to me, differs from the rest of the black men in this country because he, being raised by a white mother, deeply valued the work he put in into raising him, and rather than being a racist, chose to believe that black mothers in Chicago were putting the same amount of work to raise their black boys. Donald Trump, and Hillary Clinton, believed in no such thing; to believe in Clinton's trust of black motherhood would be a monstrous ask of any colored person in this country. Trump, having seen through this, was completely able to destroy Clinton, and was prepared to do so, after he won over the Republican voter base through direct marketing tactics, a call to war against illegals and Muslims in 2016 that, unlike the Nostalgic promises of making America great again that either Obama, Bush, or Clinton promised, simply looked to the present moment for action; while many have asked how he could have usurped the Democratic party, none have yet to take a good look at how the Republicans failed at beating him in the 2016 primaries, which, much like Obama's rise to power, has to do with the myths Americans tell themselves about what it means to be a good citizen: if all our politicians are corrupt, why are we, as individuals, Donald Trump proposed to the American public, not allowed to do the same? If they are allotted corruption on our behalf, why would not choose to endorse a man to embody that corruption for us, not simply to own the libs, but to prove that their corruption, only dressed up in gender based identity politics, simply had no meaning in a society where our young girls are cutting themselves and getting addicted to prescription pills because of the porn addictions our sons now had. Who is the Democratic party without Donald Trump looming in the background, a culmination of the sins they had kept in their closets, not for any other reason than to, like the rest of the country, rely on the image and idea of the black man in America so they could forget of King's death?

Trump, in both cases, was a response to the failed politics of the Clinton family, both in tariff policy and in immigration, but never the national debt. Trump promised to actively build a wall and fight terrorism, precisely making up for the fact that the Republicans he fought against had no threat, as Bush did, that Obama rectified, to fight against, known as the so-called "black" problem of America. Since no racial insults could be hurled at Obama, it was hard to hurl them at black America once more, and once this so called "problem" solved itself in the public eye, its material conditions were met and subsequently silenced by the Democratic establishment, only to be met, twice, by Trump: in 2016, as a fresh faced candidate that knew in moments what he needed to say to defeat Hillary Clinton, and whose intelligent but mommas boys Republican political opponents were still too entrenched in Republican Party politics, loyalism, and corruption to be easily trusted by the American public, and the second time, in 2024, when he simply won out of his political opponent, Kamala Harris', simple inability to explain to her children what was happening to the country she was helping to govern and create. Donald Trump, after all, tells his children the exact same thing he tells the American people: that it was those damned illegals. This, of course, must always overlook the fact that this has very little of anything to do with what illegal immigrants have done or did and everything to do with the fact the Democratic Party, now no longer racist, simply sees all Americans as expendable as the whole country was believed only black Americans to be. This too, however, obscures the much more troubling reality of American life: that no one, not a single person, has become a better person through the American way of life, and in the most cases, has simply become more cowardly, for not only have the old beguiled the young, but the old in need have no young people to protect them.

It is this didactic, that of the public and private so-called white identity of American life that was, in large part due to the race riots of 2020, replaced by the prive-public liberal identity of so-called black life; how true or accurate the public view of black Americans is, in relation to the private or lived experiences of black Americans in America, is precisely the new divide between the Democratic and Republican party: so-called leftists, which rely on this public view of an imagined black America, a black America that, as so far as I am concerned, no one has ever truly lived in and perhaps lives only on social media, are constantly coming into contact with Trump supporters who do not need such an identity as they did before Obama's election - with the cold war now over, the right and left identities that also coincided with the two largest white world powers worldwide, Russia and the United States, were left vacuous in ways unexpected to political pundits who still imagine, as in some way, contemporary American leftists do, that being a leftist also means being aligned with the USSR and its antisemitic regime; instead, the decoupling of America from Israel is the new so-called leftist movement, precisely because of the inability on the part of Americans to condone or even reconcile with the 2020 race riots: if black Americans could burn down every major American city in the name of "freedom", why couldn't HAMAS do the same?

I myself was caught inside this paradigm for the first 18 or so years of my life in the United States, living constantly in between the racial labels of American society without ever properly ever fitting into any - a Venezuelan, as far as white people were concerned, was not white, and as black people were concerned, not black either. It was this reality that led me to, hungering for an answer as to the so-called Latino identity and question in America, enroll in a program my school offered that while originally known as the African American Scholar Program, later on had Latino tacked on in between to be renamed as the African American Latino Scholars Program. While the "white" world was having a gender war between "democracy" and Christianity, that is to say, were fighting over the nature of Christiniaty, a world I was never included in, I sought out other options as to what exactly my place in the country was, or, more accurately, why it had yet failed to find, or create, one for me in the first place.

I lived in one of the most affluent parts of Boston, and by far one of the most "educated" parts of the country - how the Jews that I lived in defined education exactly, or their relationship to black people, and for that matter, me or my family, always seemed to have very little to do with lived reality and everything to do with perception; despite spending what today must have been millions of dollars in racial and feminist initiatives, this did not stop my black friends from trying to commit suicide, my first girlfriend, who was poor and brown, from cutting herself, or any of the white girls I had crushes on from not living with some kind of body dysmorphia whether anorexia, belemia, or otherwise. Being Latino in this kind of town, there was little I could say to an American, white or black, regarding my identity; for the most part, I took on what today is considered edgy or racist humor as my own, mostly, looking back on it, and if I am being charitable to myself, because I saw the meaninglessness, and the kind of joke, that the white man is and was: why he wished to kill me, or his daughters, while paying to educate us to protect his own sense of purity, made it so that despite growing up with two best friends, both of whom were Jewish, and whose families taught me of organic snacks, costco, Calvin and Hobbes, and another whole myriad of American values, there was always a massive gap between our lived realities. By middle school, I identified myself as a freak, a nerd, a loser, against the jocks and athletes who wanted to date the rich white girls from the school; perhaps all I was doing was finding a way myself to become popular at the expense of the kids I thought weirder, more unsightly, and freakier to my own. I never found myself beautiful, or truly believed I could get a girlfriend; the idea that a girl would be attracted to me was repulsive in itself.

That is to say, that in addition between the massive gap in lived experience between the students in all of AP and honors classes and I, and the very real reality that there may have been simply no place for me in their world, as a man, not as someone subservient to them, this reality was just as far off, and in many ways, continues to be far off from any of the black Americans I attended high school with, particularly those inside of the Scholars program, many of whom were part of busing projects that, shipping kids from different parts of Boston to different schools, were meant to forcefully integrate students to promote diversity. Originally created in the 1970s by a man from my hometown, the busing program incited race riots in the 1970s in a different part of the city: most the black and students at my school were "urban", if you can even call Boston, as a city,]"urban", in relation to the other massive ghettos of black Americans that exist throughout the country: for the most part, they merely succumbed to the definitions white Americans had of them. I never managed to make meaningful relationships with the majority of them, considering how much they seemed to hate the "white" culture which I loved: classic rock, Pink Floyd, and the Beatles. They treated professors they saw as too soft with an incredible amount of disrespect and were for the most part borderline illiterate; I think if I had not been so scared of them, considering their tough and somewhat violent demeanors, I might have been able to feel comfortable enough around them to have fostered meaningful friendships. Most were athletes and the majority of the time, as I have come to expect from black Americans, were more troubled with finding ways to have sex with the white girl everyone at the school fawned over rather than protect or stand up for any of their own. Once, during a Scholar program class in high school, the darkest skinned girl of the class, having watched a documentary about how dark skin black women in American society find that men outside of their community found them more beautiful than the ones within it, shared that she cried at her home that day, broken hearted as to if she was ever going to find love within the confines of black America. We had been friends for a short period during a school trip to Costa Rica; in that country, free from racial paradigms, we were free to interact with one another in ways we never could in Brookline; once back in the United States, I retreated into myself once more, knowing full well my place in American society. Nevertheless, most of the kids I went to high school remember me as being "mad white" - I could probably divulge into racist stereotypes at this point, but we were all too young to be judged. Usually, that just was a street way of saying "Ernesto's not interested in getting girls."

"I knew a blond girl in the village a long time ago, and eventually, we never walked out of the house together. She was far safer walking the streets alone than when walking with me. A brutal and humiliating fact which thoroughly destroyed whatever relationship this girl and I might have been able to achieve. This happens all the time in America, but Americans have yet to realize what a sinister fact this is, and what it says about them. When we walked out in the evening, then, she would leave ahead of me, alone. I would give about five minutes, and then I would walk out alone, taking another route, and meet her on the subway platform. We would not acknowledge each other. We would get into the subway car, sitting at opposite ends of it, and walk, separately, through the streets of the free and the brave, to wherever we were going... a friend's house, or the movies."[38]

-James Baldwin

Perhaps I did not yet realize it, and I certainly was too afraid to make the kind of jokes at colored people's expenses in front of the black kids I went to school with, but I was slowly making my way to the conclusion that despite what both black and white people told me, there is, as far as I am concerned, no difference between black and white culture: while both may have found different styles to meet America, black or white, the only thing I could, and can today, be assured of, from both black and white America, is that both feel comfortable with the degradation, whether in public, or in private, of the kind of black girl that told us in class who told us she broke down crying because of the color of her skin, the same kind of woman that, until this day, is expected to lay down her life, both for the community that disowned her and the community that caused them to disown her. This too, is what continues to confound what black Americans always try to reassure me about themselves and so-called "black" culture: not only did both black and white look down on us for being from the third world, and, having accepted the labels white America put on them as their own, expect me to do the same, but, moreover, that I have yet to meet more than a handful of black women in my life who, earnestly, remind me of Sexxy Red; but every single black woman I went to high school with, to this day, was captured by Billie Holiday, a woman who seemingly, much like the darkskinned black girls of my high school, were disowned by the entirety of the men of their country, writ large.

It was, in any case, still 2016, and only a few years before 2020 and the race riots would come to pass; having left for California my freshman year of college, I came back with a reinvigorated pride in myself and my identity, only to find out that once regaining this sense of self worth, I had not had remaining a single person from my pre-college life interested in it. Reading Iceberg Slim's <u>Pimp</u> during quarantine that year with my parents and older sister, and a stay at our home by my older brother, I was spurred on by a binge watching of old Dave Chapelle stand up specials to, as the rest of the country did, go out and "protest" the murders of George Floyd, Breonna Taylor, and the other victims of police brutality leading up that gave the BLM movement its infamy years before. At my high school, a rally was held in front of the main building in the same vain when a student heading to Cornell called one of the black students in the scholars program alongside me an "African American Scholar Ass NIGGER" on a Snapchat video. I believe they were both part of the crew team - the student who called the other student a nigger was, for the most part, doing it for comical purposes, not to silence him or something else along those lines. In any case, the video was leaked and none of the black students found it funny - I skipped class that day to attend, and today I wonder if when I told my friends I only went to skip class if I was saying so to protect my so-called integrity in the face of my "whiter" friends. Whatever they were protesting, from the vantage point I have today, was seemingly nothing else than the idea to have their suffering, or their identities, recognized - the idea, it seemed, of having their own schools, autonomy, or a unified political front was, as is the case today with the majority of demonstrations in America, seemingly non-existent: the condemnation and denial of suffering was enough to march.

Having sold marijuana brownies in High School, I ran into some of these students in the same demonstrations a few years later in 2020 that eventually would boil over into the riots; out of one of the men I remember was a black man I went to school with who told me that his friend, who stood over 6 feet and weighed over 200 pounds, blacked out fully from one of the edibles I had sold him. That, of course, was once the demonstrations in Boston quickly turned into riots. I still remember the palpable rage felt in the black community that day and the subsequent tension between every single member or spectator that day and the police. Marching from near downtown to Boston Common, I first met up with my white homeboy and later his girlfriend, who was accompanied by her friends, on the train ride over. Millions of Americans had come together that day in a strange sense of justice much worse, looking back on it today, than the Palestine encampments from four years later: if you polled the protesters, I doubt the majority of us could have named a combined total of 3 speeches made by Shabbaz or Dr. King. We marched simply in solidarity with ourselves, in a combined and total ideal of interpersonal freedom at the expense of the black community, who despite having "led" us into the event, were themselves only pushed to do so by the cowardice of their own leaders, Angela Davis and the like. The streets of Boston filled with so-called Americans as, in the midst of a global pandemic, "essential workers" in Boston hospitals, who in some ways, profit most desperately throughout the nation from the despair of black America and the rest of the country, its population and its ability to be exploited for drugs and mental health services, cheered us on from the windows of Boston's medical industry. 4 years later, this industry would come to rule the city alongside the lifestyles of those who profit from it: the riots, having destroyed all so-called middle class businesses in the heart of the city, left a void to filled by corporate entities which razed and destroyed the city that, despite being known as racist to some, I loved. It was this ideology that would soon come along with it Matcha, Dubai chocolate, Boba tea, and rich Chinese that would live the American dream at the expense of Americans themselves: whether or not this can even be attributed to black Americans themselves challenges all the assumptions Americans hold true about themselves, and their day to day lives, day in, and day out. By nightfall the violence would begin: the majority of black cowards there who would never rise to save their own community without a pass from the federal government to enact this violence assured everyone there, especially the white girls who cheered each other on writing BLM with spray cans on the walkways of the Boston Common, that if we were not there amongst the masses of black bodies, ready to "lay our lives down" for the cause, we should just go home. Protesters began throwing water bottles at police cruisers while my friend's girlfriend's friends thought to themselves if they would look cute in their protesting outfits for their instagrams:

whether or not I yet knew it, they too were looking to be "accepted" by black America to be seen as cool, even if no one attending the protest, neither black nor white, had any principles to stand upon that could remain triumphant in the wake of the violence.

The looting began soon after, nightfall cued in by police in riot gear zoning off the parts of the city they would let Americans loot and the parts they chose to save, being, for the most part, residential sectors of Boston's downtown that would soon become unaffordable, both materially, to those without the renting power, and morally, to those with it. Black men were seen running out of Men's Warehouses and other high end fashions stores that would never again hold popularity in American life as the nouveau riche of the country decided to emulate "Miami" style streetwear in the coming years as high end hats and fine garments rolled out of broken storefront windows like tumbleweeds in the Old West. From afar, I heard one man scream out the sizes of pants he had stolen and was trying to resell - one of the white girls we were with, to my dismay, and despite being envious of me for having rich parents but living such a privileged lifestyle and wasting it on being a 21st century white whore instead of doing her homework in school, had gone into a liquor store to steal vodka and cosplay indie sleaze. When I think of women like her, I feel such an urge to violence I wonder if maybe Allah had a point for stating that some women need to be beaten - like it would later become commonplace in black America, it seemed she was taking this moment to engage in behavior that would let her "go viral". When we reunited, she told me of a black man who was walking around with stolen Jordans, who, from behind, had a man jump over him and grab a box of shoes amidst the tower he held, looted from a local department store - we were approaching Chinatown now and a group of Dominicans or Puerto Ricans had blared into the street on dirtbikes and were shooting off fireworks into the sky, the sparks and embers of which rattled and beat against the skyscrapers of Boston's downtown. Seeing a local liquor store get looted, I looked at my friend's girlfriend and decided to go in and rob it with her - trying to restrain myself to some kind of morality, the only thing I could steal that I could not myself afford or know where to buy was a cardboard cutout of a girl holding a Soju bottle that, in the wind of Boston that night, flared like a sail in the midst of a tempest. Before then, however, in the midst of the chaos, standing in the midst of the violence, were two older black women approaching their 30's.

We were standing next to to a Walgreens in the process of being looted by young black teens and a group of white and Asian anarchists in "rioting" gear and ski googles - when I stated, out loud, I think the protest is over, an older black man walked by me and said "Yup". Young black kids with no guidance or leadership, no older than 14, were taking baseball bats to windows in the name of "freedom" - it is hard, in this moment, for me not to, in some strange sense of humility, laugh at the mere innocence, and furthermore, cowardice of the night. Seizing their moment to display their so-called black masculinity, men resorted to "threats" so low against so-called American democracy that they were stealing bags of chips from the local Walgreens. As I spoke with one of the black women who was barred from entering the side street where her apartment entrance resided, having been closed off by the police to avoid the destruction of the residential area, we got to know each other through small talk. She was a graduate student and had a child at home - she offered me vapes to buy that she sold in order to afford herself an education. The father, it seemed, was nowhere to be found, not in her home, in her life, or in the streets that day to guide the destructive youth beside me to greatness. As we stood together wondering just why anyone would need to loot a Walgreens, especially in Boston, where the urban poverty seen in the likes of other cities such as Baltimore is almost nowhere to be found, she asked me if I could go into the store and get some baby wipes for her child. Fearing the shards of glass, I asked the white and Asian anarchists to do so for me - they came out with them, in a mix of adrenaline and fear, and threw them at me. Picking them up from off the street, I handed them to her, only for her to feel bad for stealing - she slipped a few dollars underneath the automatic sliding doors that were not destroyed by the rioters in hopes someone would pick them up later on.

Holding the Soju cutout between my arms, an urban white man and his girlfriend looked at me in shock and asked why I would ever need that, not judgingly, but in jest. The woman and her friend from before were a further ways up from us smoking a blunt to pass the time - later on, I would fantasize about being her boyfriend. In the meanwhile, the Americans that had looted the liquor store were popping bottles of Champagne and spraying it throughout the street while some jumped on the roofs of their cars while "Coronao Now" by Lil' Pump and El Alfa played. Rather than a protest, it seemed more like a massive party I could not invite myself to - I stood at the sidelines, with my white friends, holding my cardboard cutout. From afar, a black man in front of a flaming dumpster held a cardboard sign that had "BLM" written on it. Journalists came to take a picture of this "historic" moment that I doubt has yet to make it into any history textbooks - the Rodney King riots barely even are. Looking at the moment with jest, and tired of holding the cutout, I threw it into the fire. One of the kids with us, a Mexican boy who was in the Scholars program with me, screamed at me, "That's racist!" while I did so.

The white girl who looted the liquor store before, at this point, had disappeared - drunk, she simply stated she was walking home, and, furthermore, was let to do so by her friends in the middle of a massive American race riot. Worrying for her safety, I tried to convince our group to find her, but before then, we would come into contact with two black kids from our high school. One was a darkskin black girl who I was personally afraid of - she was of strong character and was a walking stereotype of the colored girls in American schools that come to school late with long acrylic fingernails and iced coffee in the mornings, which she did in our junior year standardized tests. We had been assigned to the same classrooms. The black boy there was similarly disinterested in education but still somewhat passionate for racial justice - why the two could not be met in unison is something that still strikes me as confusing, considering in my junior year history class my professor taught us of Bessie Smith and the Black Panthers, and artist and movement that I would study, thoroughly, out of my own volition. They had both shown up to a house party of mine one year, parties I seldom threw - the girl seemed interested in me but was clearly uncomfortable by the whiteness of the environment, choosing to sit outside alongside the boy on the sidewalk of the white neighborhood my family lived in. Part of me wanted to tell them, in that moment, that I needed them to come inside, knowing there was a much higher likelihood of the police coming to my house that night if my neighbors saw black people in the street, regardless of what they were doing. They simply chose to leave the party. That night, however, much like the black grad student I had met, the girl was left to her own devices as the black kid from my high school chose to loot the city instead of going home alongside her to make sure she got there safely - much like the other black gur from my high school I met that day, it simply seemed they were there to act bad and steal so they could go back to their college dormitories afterwards and tell girls about it to get laid.

Breaking off from them, I called my sister to get a ride home. Before she arrived, I convinced our group to find the girl who had decided to walk home - coming across her, she was in the midst of speaking to a homeless black man on the street. Breaking up their conversation, I had assumed the worst intentions and was fearful he was trying to rape her or something else dirty that a homeless man would do, alone, with a young 18 year girl while police were busy trying to contain riots in other parts of the city. Still in contact with the black kid who had gone to loot, police officers were mobilizing around different parts of downtown while he relayed to us that he had gone into a department store to steal some Louboutin shoes, famous in rap songs, nicknamed "red bottoms". Having grown up on Drake and the like, I can only assume because they could not afford them they still considered themselves poor, despite attending some of the best public schools in the entire country. My sister picked us up and dropped everyone off at their homes - a few weeks later, a friend told me of a girl he met at the beach who carried a golden and diamond necklace she had stolen like a war trophy during the "George Floyd" riots. It is only ironic that a man who led such a despicable lifestyle would lead to riots that invoked something of the same - in a few years, no one would speak of the spectacle, let alone black Americans, who, since then, have done nothing to organize their communities or meaningfully address the problems plaguing them. Fearing another set would break out, the country decided it would be more moral to let black people kill each other than to have white people kill them - decidedly, it seems, that the only time the loss of a colored life matters in the West is when they are killed by Jews in Zion.

Laying the foundation for the political divide to come, one fully harnessed by the January 6th rioters, Americans would spend the next 4 years never addressing or even to trying to describe such an insurmountable problem as the 2020 race riots: the American class divide worsened, in large part due to the Ukraine War, and the only thing Americans could defend, as part of Western civilization, was their ability to put transgender women in women's sports. In the complete absence of any conversation, D.E.I. lectures ensured that no such tragedy would occur again: black American men, not having to be held responsible to any standard except that of so-called white liberalism, meaning never Martin Luther King or el-Hajj Malik el-Shabbaz, let alone Fannie Lou Hammer, all of whom were wrongfully removed from American history, were left in limbo as the despair and conditions of the ghetto only worsened. In their absence, Americans decided that the only idea they were comfortable investing in is best exemplified by Kai Cenat: black American men can, and should, do or be anything, except role models, but most of all, love black women.

Perhaps it is in the complete absence of this statement in the public sphere that gave rise to the term "black excellence" and the subsequent media that followed it. "Black" products were propagated throughout the internet and in the entertainment industries not as symbols of creative expressions, but much like in the days of slavery, as investments. Podcasts such as "The Shop" appeared throughout the internet, each one bringing together successful black people to talk, namely, about being successful; what then, is not the point of shows like The Shop on YouTube, if not only to gather together black artists through the stereotypes about black culture that white companies feel comfortable investing in, such as the idea of a barbershop, but if and only if that barbershop can be elevated far from the promises of the despair of the ghetto, and, furthermore, removed far enough from the lunacy of gang based entertainment podcasts such as No Jumper so much so that they despise one another? Is not the only black aspect of social life not possible to invest into the black family, one completely barred from American social life unless put on as spectacle for the rest of America to ogle into, and furthermore, as something to be celebrated precisely because it is not the norm? Are we not distracting ourselves from this possibility, that of the spectacle of success being in the generations forthcoming, rather than the idea of success being defined as that of being brought together by sponsors based along racial lines, or, in their rejection, of black Americans brought together into anti-anti-racist coalitions on conservative talk shows for the same but different reasons, namely being, finding black sponsors for non-black owned products to make both sides of the racial isle comfortable consuming said products? Who then, are these media spectacles for? JID fans, who are and have almost always been white and suburban? Migos fans, who have generally been split amongst suburban COD fans and Atlanta gangster rap aficionados? What is the culmination of these DEI efforts, if not one massive apology to black women from both sides of the racial aisle, to simply state, we will never stand up for you? What has D.E.I. done for the black community, if not help them organize to stay disorganized, and furthermore, to force the entirety of the country to convince young men to look up to gangster rappers to make up for the fact Thomas Jefferson, and his descendants, black and white alike, have yet to find any value in Sally Hemmings?

"*Here was an experiment, under the most favorable conditions, of the powers of intellect without conscience. Never was such a leader so endowed, and so weaponed; never leader found such aids and followers. And what was the result of this vast talent and power, of these immense armies, burned cities, squandered treasures, immolated millions of men, of this demoralized Europe? It came to no result. All passed away, like the smoke of his artillery and left no trace. [Napoleon] left France smaller, poorer, feebler, than he found it; and the whole contest for freedom was to be begun again. The attempt was, in principle, suicidal. France served him with life, and limb, and estate, as long as it could identify its interest with him; but when men saw that after victory was another war; after the destruction of armies, new conscriptions; and they who had toiled so desperately were never nearer to the reward,—they could not spend what they had earned, nor repose on their down-beds, nor strut in their chateaux,—they deserted him. Men found that his absorbing egotism was deadly to all other men. It resembled the torpedo, which inflicts a succession of shocks on any one who takes hold of it, producing spasms which contract the muscles of the hand, so that the man cannot open his fingers; and the animal inflicts new and more violent shocks, until he paralyzes and kills his victim. So, this exorbitant egotist narrowed, impoverished, and absorbed the power and existence of those who served him; and the universal cry of France, and of Europe, in 1814, was, "enough of him;" "assez de Bonaparte."*

It was not Bonaparte's fault. He did all that in him lay, to live and thrive without moral principle. It was the nature of things, the eternal law of man and of the world, which baulked and ruined him; and the result, in a million experiments, will be the same. Every experiment, by multitudes or by individuals, that has a sensual and selfish aim, will fail. The pacific Fourier will be as inefficient as the pernicious Napoleon. As long as our civilization is essentially one of property, of fences, of exclusiveness, it will be mocked by delusions. Our riches will leave us sick; there will be bitterness in our laughter; and our wine will burn our mouth. Only that good profits, which we can taste with all doors open, and which serves all men."

-Ralph Waldo Emerson, "Napoleon"

The Democratic party, now in shambles because it, alongside the rest of this country, has yet to answer this question, is decidedly without a voice or identity: what the Republican party will do after Trump' departure is another question no has yet had the courage to ask (I personally think Barron will become the youngest president in American history - especially so if he teams up with a man like Nick Fuentes). This question, which cannot be understated, has nevertheless remained a far off promise in the land of promised sorrows - as the country enters into a state of perpetual grief, perhaps the only thing it can now assure itself is not that it would not like to be black, but that it would not like to be Venezuelan. H1-B visas, which were a point of contention in the 2016 Republican primary, much like Ukraine was in the 2008 presidential debate, have seemingly been removed from the conversation as well; children, having been taught to endorse the race riots, did the same to HAMAS, grotesquely, for I have yet to find an example of white women kidnapped or raped by the direct actions of either Malcolm, or Martin. So despite everything that has been said, DEI and Charlie Kirk are the same thing, an explanation of white supremacy to their children, but never a reconciliation, or vision for the future, born from our own history. Both sides, in some ways, are what white, college educated white women want men to be like: to reject the "white man" but never to critique the liberal white woman's place as the upholder of virtue in society - one wants black men to be like white male liberals, and the other wants white men to be like white male liberals, while conservatives hope to reject this promise of prosperity altogether - regardless, the structure of American liberalism is beginning to collapse and the despair felt across the Western world only accumulates every hour while it does so.

"*The priest does not say, said the judge. Nihil dicit. But the priest has said. For the priest has put by the robes of his craft and taken up the tools of that higher calling which all men honor. The priest also would be no godserver but a god himself. [...]*

Your heart's desire is to be told some mystery. The mystery is that there is no mystery. "
-Cormac McCarthy, Blood Meridian

NOTES

1. Marv Wolfman, *Batman* No. 447, pencils by Jim Aparo (New York: DC Comics, May 1990).

2. Christina Kiaer, *Imagine No Possessions: The Socialist Objects of Russian Constructivism* (Cambridge, MA: MIT Press, 2005), 53.

3. Christina Kiaer, *Imagine No Possessions: The Socialist Objects of Russian Constructivism* (Cambridge, MA: MIT Press, 2005), 53.

4. Cormac McCarthy, *Blood Meridian, or the Evening Redness in the West* (New York: Vintage International, 1992).

5. F. Scott Fitzgerald, *The Great Gatsby* (New York: Scribner, 2004).

6. F. Scott Fitzgerald, *The Great Gatsby* (New York: Scribner, 2004).

7. Cormac McCarthy, *Blood Meridian, or the Evening Redness in the West* (New York: Vintage International, 1992).

8. Friedrich Nietzsche, *Beyond Good and Evil*, trans. Helen Zimmern (Project Gutenberg, 2003), https://www.gutenberg.org/ebooks/4363.

9. *Fallout: New Vegas*, developed by Obsidian Entertainment (Rockville, MD: Bethesda Softworks, 2010), video game.

10. Fabian Valdez, *Writing Advice from Matt Stone & Trey Parker @ NYU | MTVU's "Stand In,"* YouTube video, 6:01, posted January 25, 2017, https://www.youtube.com/watch?v=vGUNqq3jVLg.

11. Akira Toriyama, *Akira Toriyama's Manga Theatre*, trans. Kumar Sivasubramanian (San Francisco: VIZ Media,

2008).

12. Junji Ito, *Uzumaki*, trans. Yuji Oniki (Los Angeles: VIZ Media, 2008).

13. Gaming Historian, *The Story of R.O.B. the Robot*, YouTube video, 12:51, posted March 16, 2018, https://www.youtube.com/watch?v=w2FuHErzhVE.

14. Masahiro Sakurai, *Squeeze and Release [Game Essence]*, YouTube video, 7:44, posted September 4, 2022, https://www.youtube.com/watch?v=TYh5SJb5gWk&list=PLgKCjZ2WsVLScUWJZ7ppkHGlCUIXEj5Io&index=2.

15. DidYouKnowGaming, *Satoshi Tajiri: How Pokémon Was Made - Did You Know Gaming Ft. Furst,* YouTube video, 10:14, posted November 16, 2019, https://www.youtube.com/watch?v=G5aBg6GFufI.

16. James Baldwin, "Many Thousands Gone," *The New Yorker*, November 8, 1959.

17. Roland Barthes, "The Blue Guide," in *Mythologies*, trans. Annette Lavers (New York: Hill and Wang, 1972), 65-69.

18. Anna Wilson, "Fan Fiction and Premodern Literature: Methods and Definitions," *Transformative Works and Cultures* 36 (2021), https://doi.org/10.3983/twc.2021.2037.

19. James Baldwin, *Notes of a Native Son* (Boston: Beacon Press, 1955).

20. XXL, "DMX: Here I Am," *XXL Mag*, March 14, 2008, https://www.xxlmag.com/dmx-here-i-am/.

21. System Stories. *Pharrell & Marc Jacobs on Collaboration, Personal Style and Louis Vuitton | System Stories.* YouTube video. Posted February 29, 2024. https://www.youtube.com/watch?v=qOJIlCNPnrE.

22. UChicago Institute of Politics, *Trad Wives & Alpha Males: Gender Relations in the Blender,* YouTube video, posted February 11, 2025, https://www.youtube.com/watch?v=hXb2KlUMBpI&t=3562s.

23. Cormac McCarthy, *Blood Meridian, or the Evening Redness in the West* (New York: Vintage International, 1992).

24. Johnathan Bi, *Nietzsche's Warnings for Modern Man | UChicago's Robert Pippin,* YouTube video, posted July 12, 2024, https://www.youtube.com/watch?v=-oGqcvrGURc&t=752s.

25. u/DefiantPosition, "Plato, Aristotle, and Diogenes' Opinions on Whether...," *Reddit*, r/Animemes, June 27, 2017, https://www.reddit.com/r/Animemes/comments/6zuvbm/plato_aristotle_and_diogenes_opinions_on_whether/#lightbox.

26. Anonymous, *Disposable Soldier (Diary of a RU Mobik) - Tour 1,* translation courtesy of Cofi Anon, accessed April 24, 2025, https://files.catbox.moe/34fuhc.txt.

27. Anonymous, *Disposable Soldier (Diary of a RU Mobik) - Tour 1,* translation courtesy of Cofi Anon, accessed April 24, 2025, https://files.catbox.moe/34fuhc.txt.

28. Fyodor Dostoyevsky, *The Gambler,* trans. C. J. Hogarth (Project Gutenberg, May 2000), https://www.gutenberg.org/ebooks/2197.

29. Cormac McCarthy, *Blood Meridian, or the Evening Redness in the West* (New York: Vintage International, 1992).

30. Cormac McCarthy, *Blood Meridian, or the Evening Redness in the West* (New York: Vintage International, 1992).

31. Anonymous, *Disposable Soldier (Diary of a RU Mobik) - Tour 1,* translation courtesy of Cofi Anon, accessed April 24, 2025, https://files.catbox.moe/34fuhc.txt.

32. "*I Am Not Your Negro (2016) – Transcript.*" *Scraps from the Loft.* Accessed July 29, 2025. https://scrapsfromtheloft.com/movies/james-baldwin-i-am-not-your-negro-transcript/.

33. *From The Anxiety to The Anatomy of Influence:*

A Conversation with Harold Bloom. YouTube video. Posted by PEN America, May 3, 2011. https://www.youtube.com/watch?v=HbZ2lUunN3I.

34. *"Controversial congresswoman Marjorie Taylor Greene filed for divorce from husband while having affair with tantric sex guru,"* Daily Mail (UK Edition), by *Daily Mail US Staff*, published February 2021 (date approximate), accessed July 29, 2025, via *Daily Mail* website.

35. *DISPOSABLE SOLDIER (diary of a RU mobik) – TOUR 2.* Translated by Cofi Anon. Catbox.moe. Accessed July 29, 2025. https://files.catbox.moe/uj2wut.txt.

36. *Katt Williams: The New War Is The Lie Vs Truth.* YouTube video. Posted by "Katt Williams – Stand Up," September 7, 2024. https://www.youtube.com/watch?v=4Ldyez5FWOE.

37. *Hunter Biden Interview.* YouTube video. Posted by "Channel 5 with Andrew Callaghan," July 21, 2025. https://www.youtube.com/watch?v=XBbkt2vYC4M.

38. *"I Am Not Your Negro (2016) – Transcript."* Scraps from the Loft. Accessed July 29, 2025. https://scrapsfromtheloft.com/movies/james-baldwin-i-am-not-your-negro-transcript/.

BIBLIOGRAPHY

Anonymous. *Disposable Soldier (Diary of a RU Mobik) - Tour 1.* Translation courtesy of Cofi
    Anon. Accessed April 24, 2025. https://files.catbox.moe/34fuhc.txt.

Baldwin, James. "Many Thousands Gone." *The New Yorker*, November 8, 1959.

Baldwin, James. *Notes of a Native Son.* Boston: Beacon Press, 1955.

Barthes, Roland. "The Blue Guide." In *Mythologies*, translated by Annette Lavers, 65-69. New
    York: Hill and Wang, 1972.

Bi, Johnathan. *Nietzsche's Warnings for Modern Man | UChicago's Robert Pippin.* YouTube
    video. Posted July 12, 2024. https://www.youtube.com/watch?v=-oGqcvrGURc&t=752s.

Daily Mail US Staff. "Controversial congresswoman Marjorie Taylor Greene filed for divorce
    from husband while having affair with tantric sex guru." *Daily Mail* (UK Edition), February 2021. Accessed July 29, 2025.

DidYouKnowGaming. *Satoshi Tajiri: How Pokémon Was Made - Did You Know Gaming Ft.*
    Furst. YouTube video, 10:14. Posted November 16, 2019. https://www.youtube.com/watch?v=G5aBg6GFufI.

Dostoyevsky, Fyodor. *The Gambler.* Translated by C. J. Hogarth. Project Gutenberg. Released
    May 2000. https://www.gutenberg.org/ebooks/2197.

Fitzgerald, F. Scott. *The Great Gatsby.* New York: Scribner, 2004.

From The Anxiety to The Anatomy of Influence: A Conversation with

Harold Bloom. YouTube
    video. Posted by PEN America, May 3, 2011. https://
    www.youtube.com/watch?v=HbZ2lUunN3I.

Gaming Historian. *The Story of R.O.B. the Robot.* YouTube video,
12:51. Posted March 16,
    2018. https://www.youtube.com/watch?v=w2FuHErzhVE.

"I Am Not Your Negro (2016) – Transcript." *Scraps from the Loft.*
Accessed July 29, 2025.
    https://scrapsfromtheloft.com/movies/james-baldwin-i-
    am-not-your-negro-transcript/.

Hunter Biden Interview. YouTube video. Posted by "Channel 5 with
Andrew Callaghan," July
    21,   2025.   https://www.youtube.com/watch?
    v=XBbkt2vYC4M.

Ito, Junji. *Uzumaki.* Translated by Yuji Oniki. Los Angeles: VIZ
Media, 2008.

Katt Williams: The New War Is The Lie Vs Truth. YouTube video.
Posted by "Katt Williams –
    Stand Up," September 7, 2024. https://www.youtube.com/
    watch?v=4Ldyez5FWOE.

Kiaer, Christina. *Imagine No Possessions: The Socialist Objects of
Russian Constructivism.*
    Cambridge, MA: MIT Press, 2005.

McCarthy, Cormac. *Blood Meridian, or the Evening Redness in the
West.* New York: Vintage
    International, 1992.

Nietzsche, Friedrich. *Beyond Good and Evil.* Translated by Helen
Zimmern. Project Gutenberg,
    2003. https://www.gutenberg.org/ebooks/4363.

Obsidian Entertainment. *Fallout: New Vegas.* Published by
Bethesda Softworks. Rockville, MD:'
    Bethesda Softworks, 2010. Video game.

Sakurai, Masahiro. *Squeeze and Release [Game Essence].* YouTube
video, 7:44. Posted
    September 4, 2022. https://www.youtube.com/watch?
    v=TYh5SJb5gWk&list=PLgKCjZ2WsVLScUWJZ7ppkHGlCUI

XEj5Io&index=2.

System Stories, *Pharrell & Marc Jacobs on Collaboration, Personal Style and Louis Vuitton |*
 System Stories, YouTube video, posted February 29, 2024, https://www.youtube.com/watch?v=qOJIlCNPnrE.

Toriyama, Akira. *Akira Toriyama's Manga Theatre.* Translated by Kumar Sivasubramanian. San
 Francisco: VIZ Media, 2008.

UChicago Institute of Politics. *Trad Wives & Alpha Males: Gender Relations in the Blender.*
 YouTube video. Posted February 11, 2025. https://www.youtube.com/watch?v=hXb2KlUMBpI&t=3562s.

u/DefiantPosition. "Plato, Aristotle, and Diogenes' Opinions on Whether..." *Reddit,* r/Animemes,
 June 27, 2017. https://www.reddit.com/r/Animemes/comments/6zuvbm/
 plato_aristotle_and_diogenes_opinions_on_whether/
 #lightbox.

Wilson, Anna. "Fan Fiction and Premodern Literature: Methods and Definitions."
 Transformative Works and Cultures 36 (2021). https://doi.org/10.3983/twc.2021.2037.

Wolfman, Marv. *Batman* No. 447. Pencils by Jim Aparo. New York: DC Comics, May 1990.

Valdez, Fabian. *Writing Advice from Matt Stone & Trey Parker @ NYU | MTVU's "Stand In."*
 YouTube video, 6:01. Posted January 25, 2017. https://www.youtube.com/watch?v=vGUNqq3jVLg.

XXL. "DMX: Here I Am." *XXL Mag.* Published March 14, 2008. https://www.xxlmag.com/dmx-here-i-am/.

Made in the USA
Middletown, DE
09 November 2025

20301043R00074